DONALD LANGOSY: THE POET'S PAINTER

First published in 2017
by Maida Vale Publishing
An imprint of Eyewear Publishing

Cover design and typeset by Edwin Smet
Printed in England by TJ International Ltd, Padstow, Cornwall

ISBN 978-1-908998-49-1

MIX
Paper from responsible sources
FSC® C013056

The editor has generally followed American spelling and punctuation at the author's request. Edited by Todd Swift and Alex Payne, with a lot of help from Edwin Smet.

WWW.EYEWEARPUBLISHING.COM

DONALD LANGOSY:

The Poet's Painter

99 poems by

ERIC SIGLER

illustrating 99 paintings

MAIDA VALE PUBLISHING

TABLE OF CONTENTS

BOOK TWO

BOOK THREE

INTRODUCTION

Since I was a small child I always knew I would be a painter, but along the way, as my intellect matured, I began to culture my inspiration in a creative petri dish, through an interest in various other artistic practices. The one practice that has continued to hold the strongest influence over me (second only to being a painter) is that of a poet.

As a freshman in high school I became aware of Ezra Pound. It was not through an introduction to his poetry, but rather one on current events. It described his release from a Washington DC mental hospital and his return to Europe. I was intrigued by Pound's presence and began researching his poetry, which to my still unsophisticated mind, was indecipherable. Perhaps I responded to some music in the words, for my understanding could not have gone beyond an intrigue in their sound.

Nevertheless, I decided to become a poet. Yet, over the remainder of my teen years and into my early twenties, I zigzagged between being either a poet or a painter, both art forms vying to dominate my attention.

In 1970, I arrived in Boston after returning from Europe. I met my first patron and, at the age of twenty-two, was given the opportunity to paint an enormous mural in his Victorian mansion. While I was still enamored by the poetic word, the creation of the mural demanded intense dedication to my love for the painted image.

Still, I was torn between the two crafts. The mural took a year to paint, after which I went to Venice, determined to meet Ezra Pound. One late afternoon on the Zattere, as a light fog began to settle in, I began walking over a footbridge. Coming up from the opposite side was the old poet. His gaze cast upon me with defiance, his eyes felt like they were drilling two black holes through me. His companion, Olga Rudge, stopped me at the top of the bridge. She asked me if I was the person leaving little watercolors outside the door to their home. Yes, I was. We spoke quietly together, Ezra Pound ignoring me and turning his attention to flirting with my wife, Elizabeth. Olga invited us to their home. But that first meeting, as remarkable as it was, was diminished several days later, when I walked into the Frari Church and was confronted by Titian's painting of *The Assumption of the Virgin*.

This was the epiphany I had been seeking. I realized that I would never be a poet, though I would always revere bards. My unexpected confrontation with Titian brought the realization that I did not think creatively in the language of words. My language was a visual one. While Ezra Pound was a remarkable linguist, I lacked the ability to see beyond my basic knowledge of English. At first I was heartbroken. Then I felt relieved by this realization that my true language was silent and wordless. Inspiration needed to be attended to visually at my easel.

So, it was settled. I was a painter. But the poet/painter connection does not end there. The poet has always been eager to herald the gifts of the painter, and the painter has always looked to the poetic vision for inspiration.

Throughout the history of the arts this relationship has persisted between the two creative forces. For instance, one of Titian's closest friends was the poet Pietro Aretino, who devoted himself to spreading praise for the painter throughout Europe.

In more recent times, there was the remarkable loyalty of poets for Pablo Picasso. Picasso, the great titan of the 20th century art world, seemed to collect poets like a war hero collected medals. The Spanish poet Jaime Sabartés was devoted to him throughout his life. During his early years in Paris, he was championed by Apollinaire, Max Jacob, Jean Cocteau, and Gertrude Stein as well as others. He continued to accumulate poets throughout his life, such as Jacques Prévert and Paul Éluard.

The poet/painter friendship has been prevalent for years. Giotto was a lifelong friend of Dante. Thomas Eakins was close to Walt Whitman. Balthus was mentored by Rilke. Manet had Baudelaire. Salvador Dalí had Federico García Lorca. Francis Bacon not only drew his influence from the poetry of TS Eliot, Ezra Pound, and WB Yeats but also maintained a close friendship with Michel Leiris. And the divine Michelangelo took it a step further by also being a poet.

As an artist, I have never felt complete without poets in my life. I was fortunate that while I was still in my twenties poets began visiting my studio. Eric Sigler was the first poet, and forty years later is still a vital force in my creative journey.

In the 1970s, Eric introduced me to his mentor, the poet Antonio Giarraputo, who became a dynamic poetic presence in my studio. Our friendship was immediate. Antonio had seen my paintings prior to our meeting, never learned my name but always longed to know the painter. And I, having heard of him from friends, had visualized him perfectly, even the sound of his voice. So upon meeting, we already felt we were close friends. Time did not seem to matter in our friendship. Although Antonio was more than twenty years older than me, missing out on each other's yesterdays was unimportant to us. We met in the present and remained there.

We both liked working through the night. Antonio would call during this time and read his current poem to me. I would describe the picture I was working on. But we could have been aliens speaking on the phone from different planets. The great admiration we had for each other's work did not really translate into a practitioner's knowledge of the actual creation of it.

Leonardo da Vinci wrote: 'And if you call painting dumb poetry, the painter may call poetry blind painting.' The poet and painter comprehend the same moment from different viewpoints. Yet, I have never seen anyone but a poet react more intensely to paintings or seem more understanding of the painter's vision.

Poets are a gift of the gods who through poetic syntax can construct visual objects out of emotions. This must be the crux of the painter/poet relationship. I have always loved the lyricism of painting, which wordlessly imbues its images with emotions and psychology. But there remains an insistence to validate these images through verbal explanation. As a young painter it seemed that I spent as much time explaining my pictures as I spent painting them. Now in my sixties, I no longer care to explain what I have intended to create sans words. I would rather turn that task over to a poet to explain it with his verbal/optical magic.

In 2001, my wife and I were in London visiting our daughters. My younger daughter brought me to the National Gallery to see my favorite painting, Titian's *Bacchus and Ariadne*. I had never seen it except in reproductions. I was immediately mesmerized by it. My daughter and wife left me and went off to view the other galleries. I do not know how long I stood looking at it. Time ceased existing. But eventually I became aware of the world outside of my mind's fixation.

I realized that standing next to me, the entire time, was another person as engaged with the painting as me. Slowly, we began to acknowledge each others' presence. We both had traveled a great distance to see Titian's masterpiece. And we both had arrived in front of it at the same time. We introduced ourselves. I was a painter from Boston, and he was a poet from Brooklyn.

Antonio had been dead for a decade, but that did not stop him from reciting one of his poems in my mind.

Album Leaf
after Ma Yuan

before the temple gate
of Yin, the Moon-son,
two burdened strangers met
and bowed in cognizance –
and silently departed
together,
                    burdenless –

– Antonio Alfredo Giarraputo

— DONALD LANGOSY

Self-Portrait with Angel, 1995 – 49"x41"

PROLOGUE – SELF-PORTRAIT WITH ANGEL

Perhaps we can encounter the multi-colored lands and be-demoned beaches of Donald's at once subterranean and celestial, whimsical and light-lit, tragic and comic cranium together, along the Rhapsode's cloud and star, moon and sunlit route, and witness live the 'Temptormation of Saint Antonio', 'The Apotheosis of Pulcinella', the thought (itself) of Donald as artiste home alone on 'Prom Night' and fantasizing, with ironic regret, what frolic he had missed. 'The Blind Fisherman' leading us with lantern through his Beach Suites, shipwrecking on Prospero's island, being lured into ecstasy by Ectoplasm, wading for hours through the seas of his studio, with clowns and mages, darlings and demons, getting lost in closets full of colorful costumes, discussing light and dark and devils and angels, serpents and apples, guilt and irreverence with Milton, drifting with the 'Boat of Poets', walking like Orpheans through sylvan scenes where zephyrs, fauns, satyrs, humans all inhabit the same forest pools below the waterfalls, where foliage-shaded light shafts through, where soft whites of the quick streams bring the light to glow. Many are the lands, allegories, planes and peoples, many are the goat-hooved and demonic, many are the angelic, most in settings more than imagined, thus more real, of which, with the Singers' help, we hope to sing!

— ERIC SIGLER

BOOK ONE

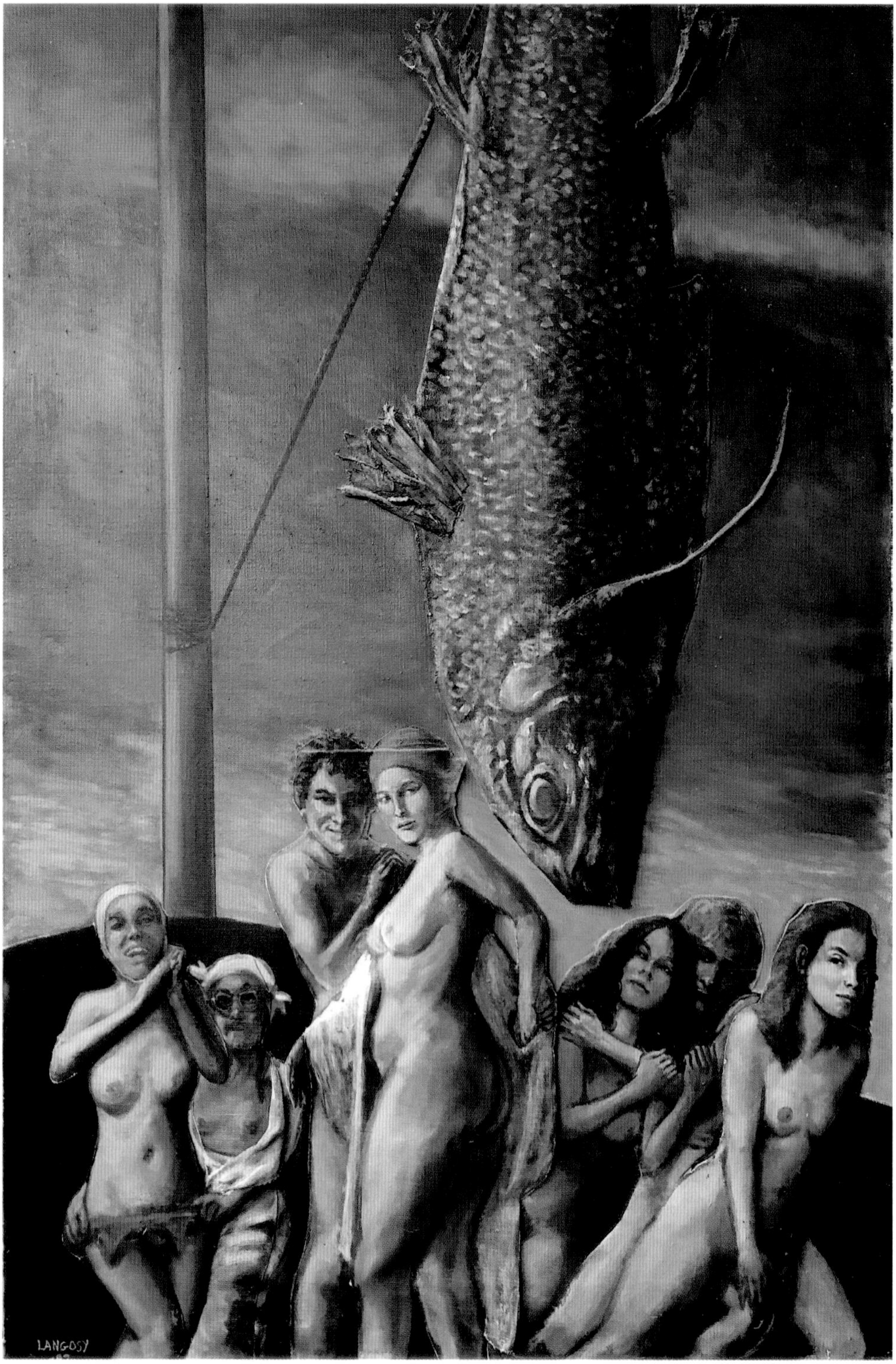

The Survivors, 1996 – 52" X 34"

I

THE SURVIVORS

The sea – bereft of fishes –
But not of breasts and thighs...
Out set we – a blue fish for a sail –
A capless tower before us –
Dead ahead: in the sunlit moonrise...
Reflections of the fish-scales

Stoke the floating phosphors:
The embers of the sea...
Out set we: the weight upon we eight
To offer to creation, as survivors,
Our awe to hear and see,
While others: all the rest, are desolate

And destroyed – incorporeal...
We are here as forms,
And with the sunlit showers
Of our consciousness, present to reveal
The maelstrom of these storms,
These joyous pysche-hours.

Perseus And Andromeda, 2004 – 32" X 25"

II

PERSEUS AND ANDROMEDA

Up from the gloaming night the brilliant sun
Shudders us from sleep, but still we dream
Of dragons, claws as fangs, the scowling sea,
Sacrifice that's chained to death's oblivion...
Perseus, son of the golden rain, winging home
From slaying the snake-haired harpy:

Marmorean Medusa, her terrible gorgon head
Strapped tight to his belt, hears Andromeda,
Chained to the sea-whipped rocks – her siren-figure
Lures her love to rescue – a love so winged –
That all the height and breadth of all phenomena
Is humming with the heartbeat of his nature...

Talon-toothed Cetus does not notice death
Is whirring like a scythe above his head –
The sword's sharp stroke encrimsoning his jowls –
A ruby rain stains the turbid wind's red breath,
Pumped by the heart enflamed by dragon blood
Yet, as her demon drowns, the turgid ocean roils.

Moby Dick, 2009 – 50" X 42"

III

MOBY DICK

Adrift at work, I'm Queequeg, Ishmael, Ahab –
Poised with harpoon upon the whaleboat bow,
Searching for Moby Dick in these dark waters,
My mind sidles through my mind as though a crab,
Seeking the answers I do not know now...
My thoughts suck deep – deep in maelstrom's whirr –

Where subterranean constructs roil the sea,
The oceans of the unknowns. The gates of Hell
Are opened for the legions of my demons
(Without the vision of conscious clarity)
Who dance like sea-foam whipped up by a spell –
Cast by the voice of Ahab in his sermons.

His passion to destroy the great white whale...
As I have hoped for reason in my questions –
The primal instincts – natural to me –
Blow like the breath of passion drives the sails.
What I seek are the winds of transformation,
Or to find my God in the heavens of the sea.

Boat Of Poets, 2009 – 46" X 51"

IV

BOAT OF POETS

Adrift upon our vessel as we pass
Floating in the drifts, a boat of poets –
Whose waking eyes are fixed
Upon the future's compass...
Their watery reflections face the past:
The times and timeless mixed

Beneath the green Orphean weave
That leans as if to listen to their silence
From the shores... that so astounds
The senses, these multi-colored leaves
Shiver gently with the touch of dance:
A painted fan upon a shifting wind.

Underneath the light the subtle moon
Throws a gold reflection from the waters
Into the vision of our passing night...
As the poets drift, I shudder to assume,
Beneath the subtle moon, our destiny and future
Are singing! Singing! Singing! Singing light!

The Blind Fisherman, 1977 – 60" X 50"

V

THE BLIND FISHERMAN

We pass along alone except the dark
That leaks its subtle shadows on our drift
Until, upon the wind, a softened light
Dances through lustrous distance to our barque...
We left the manateed waters of the poets,
Mermaids calling calling through the night,

To see this glow – follow as soft light flattens
The seamless sea. We move closer, ever closer –
The silence of the sea-swells in our ears –
Then we hear music: in it all that happens,
Has happened, or will happen: the future,
Past and present: in it which appears

A lamp held by a blind man on the shore,
And four who follow closely on the sand,
Dancing to waves of light, as seeping shadows –
That animate Picasso – are glowing in light's ore...
The Fisherman will guide us: his blind hand
Will seek survivors in today's tomorrows.

Out Of The Sea, 1995 – 25" X 18"

VI

OUT OF THE SEA

Lured by the siren lamp to the maelstrom's gyre,
The ship was left in pieces on the sea,
Twirled in its torment until it was drowned...
Yet – on the surface, underneath the stars,
The bodies floated – drifted – silently,
As quiet as a breath that has no sound.

Amphitrite stood on a shelf of rocks
That channeled waves around it to the shore...
Having saved the lives she chose to save.
Was it Li Po morphed into Young Bacchus?
Wasn't his body meant to be the anchor?
Was he drunk with a life he could not live?

They rode the Sea Horse River – in the moon,
Surprised as they looked upon the male as is...
The marvel of empathy upon their faces,
The oceans had claimed a new Endymion,
Yet – they will save this moonchild – just because
Amphitrite saved these gentle Graces.

Out Of The Sea 2, 1995 – 24" X 24"

VII

OUT OF THE SEA II

Youth was borne on the light lit by the moon
Upon the tides that washed him to the shore...
He floated by the gentle mermaid's side –
Singing to him, calling – calling to resume
His breath upon the wind – like Spenser's Calidor –
And singing to the Sirens makes them hide...

She lifts his head from the waters so that breath
Can lift again from the lifeless form he seems...
She places her hand upon his quiet chest,
As if to touch the life back from his death,
As if to bring that sleep back as a dream
Of when he'll lie again upon her breast...

Lifeless... limp... they pull him from the waters,
Using the tides that ride the waves of light,
Using the strength they give, the hope they hold...
Away – beyond sight – the Sirens' ears are shattered –
No more can they steal the moonlight from the night...
And – like his thoughts – the white-capped rivers roll.

Out Of The Sea 3, 1995 – 36" X 24"

VIII

OUT OF THE SEA III

Let's return to the gentlings of the sea
That drifts within us, as we speed along...
After Genesis – started with a sound –
Oceans bore him as the form we see
Back to our tender arms – where he belongs –
Each of us a Prometheus – unbound –

But none the more than she... the moon
Herself can make the sea a stream –
White-capped rivers of light a path
That swims in gentle waves upon the skin
That trembles in the cradle of a dream –
The Morphean light – the sea-foam birth

Of Venus... incubating in the shallow sea...
O, our skin was sweetened by the salt
And all that it preserved – our floating lives...
And so we hold his limp yet supple body,
And on our faces share our love in thought –
The tender Graces here – his spirit wives...

The Storyteller, 1982-83 – 42" X 40"

IX

THE STORYTELLER

The Rhapsode hides his lamp inside blind eyes;
Somewhere in his mind he sees the wick
Light the soft fire that glows upon the ears
That gather beneath a flight of fireflies
Which reddens the night horizon with its sparks,
That burst into flame to entertain the seers...

He moves as though a moment waits to hear
The gestures that compel his hands to move,
To simulate the rhythm of his words,
Which sing of visions evanescing here,
That dissipate, yet magnify pure love –
The hero's magma – smelted in the sword –

The tale of lovers thrust into the void
Who never heard the voice they knew again...
And songs of magic – potions that defend
The lands and seas where song would be destroyed...
We hear the sail as it listens for the wind –
We feel pure love from the Land of Neverend.

A Vision, 2003 – 26" X 22"

X

A VISION

'Dead by the waters of the sand,
Yet, in my questions – deep – as though alive...
I've suffered the intangibles of fate
That I welcomed with an open hand
To touch the terrible light that I survive –
So that my grounded feet can levitate...

What do I care of matters of the world –
Surrounded by Three Graces?
What do I care of death and life and light?
How can these paintings ever speak a word?
How can I paint the motion in their faces?
How can I move illumined through the night?

The Angels in me always meditate...
The Graces in me – forms – are always shifting...
Beyond all knowledge – knowing it is nothing –
Yet, with every stroke, it's light I animate –
The Graces or The Self or all as Wings –
Whether if sun or moon it is one thing...'

On The Sand With Printless Foot, 2011 – 36" X 36"

XI

ON THE SAND WITH PRINTLESS FOOT

In the vagaries I found my vision...
It was of myself... I was beside
The woman, less intangible than I,
Her tri-part soul melded in illusion –
Each part on the other's other side,
All upon the sand, as though the sky...

As I am committed to the ethers,
In the air, with spectral point of view,
Wondering why I came to understand
The part of me that is an antimatter –
The spirit that assimilates in you.
With conch shell of a pig's heart in her hand,

Pressed upon her womb, and beating still,
With Flora's specter holding out a rose,
With earnest hands from nowhere on her breasts,
Existing as the chosen of her will,
She smiles a smile I could not presuppose,
And brings her body closer to the rest.

Naked Vessels, 2000 – 35"X 38"

XII

NAKED VESSELS

Underneath the layers of the sea,
Where clay is made of sand and sand of light,
Where light defines the color and the depth,
Where water is made of air that seamlessly
Moves on the tides – assembles in the current –
The waves of motion as fluid as a breath,

A liquid measure – the temple of a thought –
Submerged therein, immersed and then – emerged
From an undertow that mystifies the ghosts,
Who have been where other shades have not...
Eduardo Gunkla – the bearded mesmerist –
Guides the Wooly Boheman in fantasies of mist –

Rides like a maharajah – through the oceans –
Dances like naked vessels – towards the shore.
O carry my soul in the bottom of the urn
Borne by her strength into a light of vision
Ineffable as the sea that seems the air –
The sea of fire – that immolates – and burns!

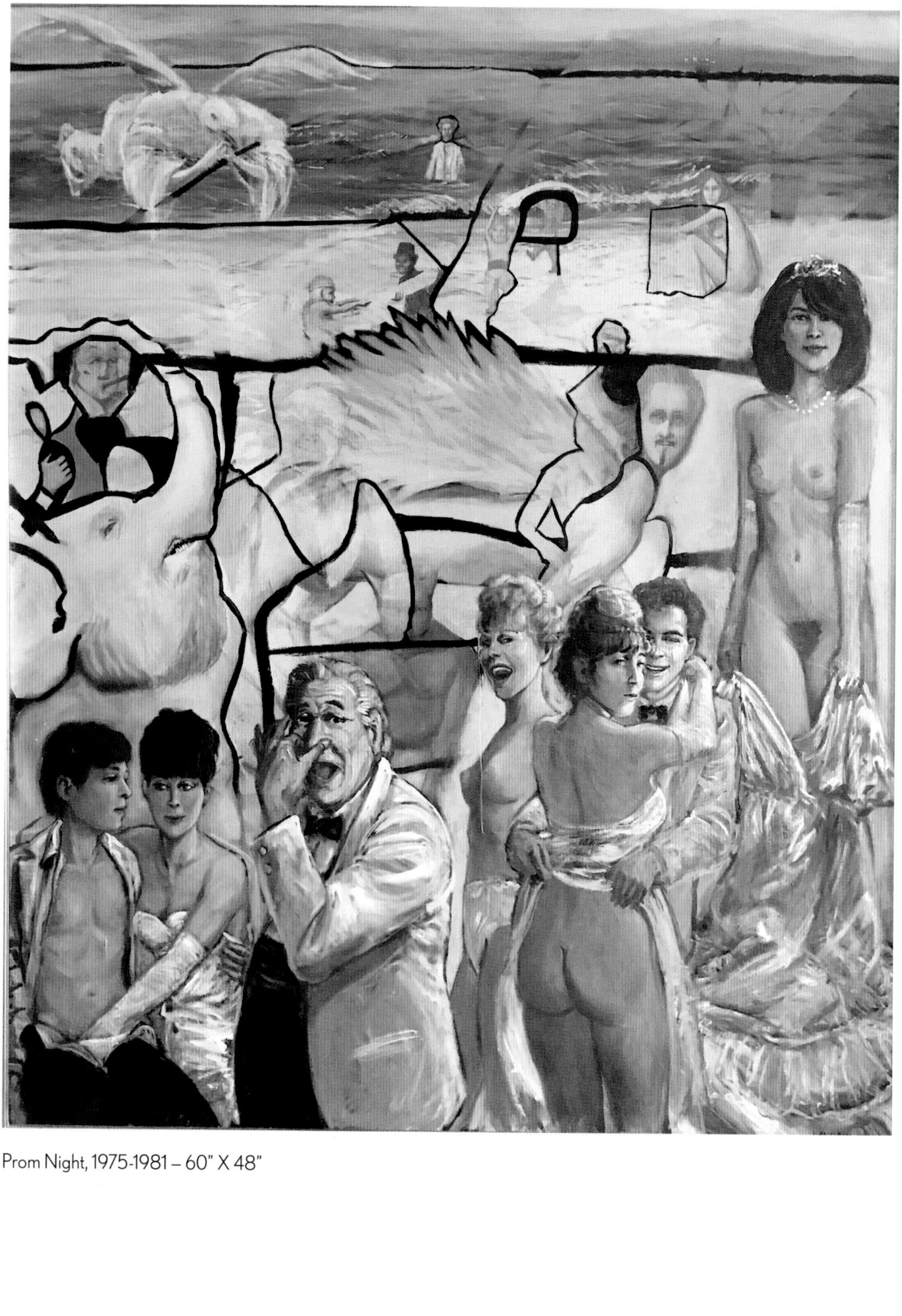

Prom Night, 1975-1981 – 60" X 48"

XIII

PROM NIGHT

We do not stop for moments – but for light...
With Mercury's speed, while the muses bless us –
Urge us to uncover – what was never there –
And yet, what was: The Queen of 'Prom Night'
On rose-gowned plinth – in confident undress,
The golden background – gilded atmosphere –

Soft upon her skin, a necklace of glowing pearls
Underlights her neck, her face, her hair –
Radiates soft white light upon her shoulders,
While buttocks, breasts and gloves, erotic girls –
(Who do not sense the Boheman dying there,
Engaging, with flirtations, fantasies and lovers)

Recede into the backdrop of all eyes...
Deep in the gilded background is a death:
The Wooly Boheman, recurrent in all dreams,
Is dying with his demons – released of all of these,
The strange transition: breathless to a breath –
So what it is it is and as it is it seems...

La Grande Prom Queen, 1985 – 40" X 30"

XIV

LA GRANDE PROM QUEEN

Let's ask the sweet seductress if the lyre,
Or any air guitar, or any tepid wind,
Can rouse her from her self-exotic state,
As clouds and sea and beach and chair
And rose-pink gown – dropped for her friends
To see – are fit to frame her – founder of all Fate –

She has the Mona Lisa in her smile –
The Grande Prom Queen – demure before the sky –
Softened by the how the when the why,
As all light's lasers feel her sultry guile,
And even though not there the sea birds cry,
And all the whispers wonder, with a sigh

If ages of undress await their fancy,
If, in the shoals of star-fish, there is light,
If annals of affection, from her rose-gloved hand,
Will touch them, or if her sea of energy
Is merely vanity as 'The Queen of Prom Night'...
We drop onto our knees upon the sand.

After The Prom, 1985 – 60" X 48"

XV

AFTER THE PROM

After the Prom, the Prom Queen and her court
Find themselves – salacious at the beach –
Looking delicious to the sun and sky –
Red with the blush of lust as they disport,
And flash the flesh that waited – each for each –
Brilliant and bright – to animate the eye...

These lovers – in the orgy of creation –
Promise the rings that circle and entice
The missions of motion, rhythms of the waves,
The cyclic yearning, moments when sensation
Explodes in the selection or the choice –
The techno-music heating up the rave.

She leans upon her lover like he leans –
Lithe and supple – like a licking fire –
Ever towards the end – the dreamy ember...
The heat that rages underneath the scene,
The passion behind the passion – the desire,
And all of that – and all of this – for her.

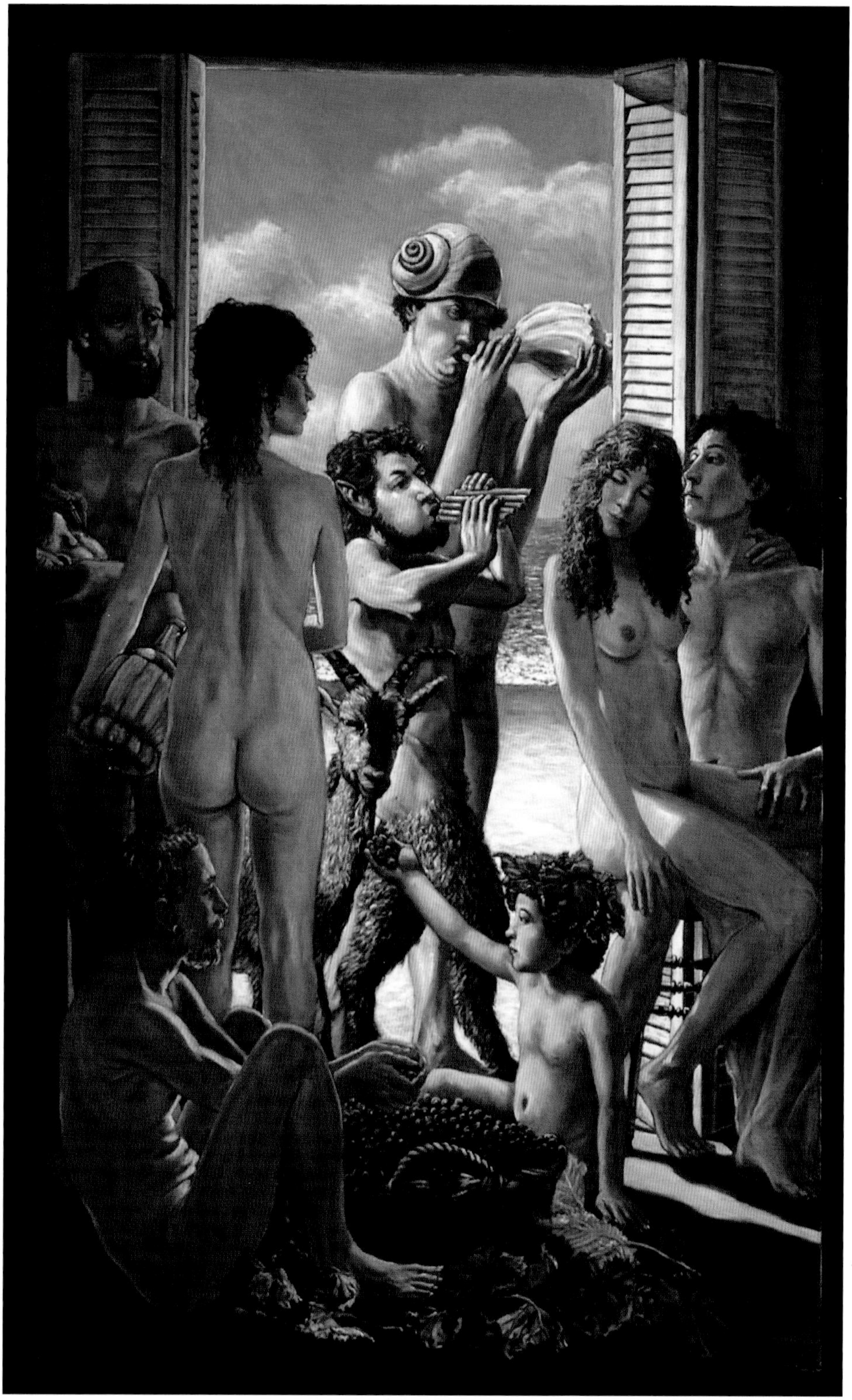

The Hour Of The Goat, 1981 – 84" X 66"

XVI

THE HOUR OF THE GOAT

Propped at a beachside bar we heard a sound,
As though Poseidon roared through a conch shell horn,
Accompanied by the high-pitched Pipes of Pan –
Even the rush of the breaking waves was drowned:
The strange cacophonous clamor
Was carried by the wind across the sand.

Then at the clam-shack door we saw the source
Of all of the confusion sounding from the breath
Blown through the ancient instruments of wind.
Then our ears were filled with Jupiter's voice
As though the spirit of God had come to earth,
Foretelling the pillars of light on Moses' head.

Pan was standing before us with Poseidon
And at his side there stood the sacred goat,
Offered the grapes that one could turn to wine,
So as we drank in the shadows of the sun
The feelings of bliss and joy began to float
Among the spirits of those who are divine.

St. Antonio Meets Two Demons In The Desert, 2014 – 37" X 36"

XVII

ST. ANTONIO MEETS TWO DEMONS IN THE DESERT

The sand has sifted to another sand –
Not the sand of sea, the sea of desert...
We're taken here as if we are diffractions
Of otherworldly light – so fast we speed –
That sand's bright crystals make our white eyes glint
With every color known – with all sensation...

The fattened friar is standing on his staff...
The demon-headed satyr comes to call...
The devil in the centaur hopes to beckon:
Summon good friar Antonio to his bath,
Where many the ripened pleasures of his downfall
Await him, in the throes of his temptation...

His sole redemption lies beneath his eyes...
In his heart he hears the treacherous tongue
Speak of flames and cloven-hooved desire,
And wonders what the dare would compromise...
If he would 'be among their cloudy trophies hung'
As carnage for their damned eternal fire!

By The Sea (with Eduardo Gunkla), 1995 – 54" X 36"

XVIII

BY THE SEA (WITH EDUARDO GUNKLA)

When we awoke we could not find the Prom Queen.
She seemed to have vanished as if from a dream.
We walked the morning clouds across the sands,
But could not find the echo of where she'd been,
As if she had drifted like Zephyr on a light beam,
Perhaps to the dreaming forests of 'The Woodlands'.

And then we met all-knowing Eduardo Gunkla –
Chill as champagne among his admiring harem –
And asked him if he knew where she is now...
Beneath the red fez, in the heat of Ra,
Eduardo told us that he didn't know when,
But that we would find her underneath a bough.

We did not recognize her – in disguise –
Out of her rose-pink gown and now half-dressed
In harem-best: a veil of sheerest silk –
Hiding her brilliant face beneath her eyes...
So we chose to follow her to the forest
To find her in the shadows of the dark.

Silenus and Prom Queen In The Woods, 1985 – 40" X 42"

XIX

SILENUS AND PROM QUEEN IN THE WOODS

The Fisherman left behind, we stumble, blind –
Sped on wings of thought, we search for shadows,
And plunge into the magic of the woods...
The leaves grow denser – on them light reclines...
The path we took – that no one ever chose –
Is just for the forest deities and gods.

Yet, the forest has a footstep and an echo...
We follow the sound, as though it is our own,
Until we hear the rustling of the Prom Queen
And find her rapt in wonder, seated solo
On a stone – a rose-pink gown upon a sylvan throne –
A cluster of sweet alyssum in her hands.

From the shades the shadow of Silenus,
Bearing his heady jar of endless wine,
Has come to offer love – enchant her with intent –
With eyes of stars, elixirs, amulets – with raucous
Potions – that stimulate the body and the mind –
Yet, she pays no heed – deep in alyssum's scent.

Clown Meets The Gods, 1977-81 – 38" X 32"

XX

CLOWN MEETS THE GODS

'Hello Pantheon, I'm Pantomime –
O Thalia, Daphne, Bacchus and Faunus,
I'm trying to act like flora in the forest.
I wonder: could you pose here? Would you mind?
I think that we can make our limbs a bush.
Thalia: take my hand... I'll touch my chest.

Daphne: place your palm upon my shoulder.
Young Bacchus, touch my skull-cap, and your chin,
Faunus, put your best puck-face right here...
I'll pose my painted nose and stand full center
(In this way you can see the god therein...
In the event that was not crystal clear).

I am no poseur – although I am posing –
I'm just a synesthete, so I am you:
We share the selfsame roots... and as we climb
Our branching thoughts, I think I am supposing
That this humble clown is now a god: Mon Dieu!
(Pssst... I'm told that my expression is sublime.)'

Clown Spends A Happy Weekend With Bacchus, 1978 – 35" X 27"

XXI

CLOWN SPENDS A HAPPY WEEKEND WITH BACCHUS

Come, let us drink the Assyrian wine,
In earthen goblets from an earthen urn.
The Meliae, born of blood from the sack
Of Uranus, are engaging, or supine.
Our grape-eyed clown thinks 'everything's divine',
Which implies: when drinking do not think –

Drunk for days with celebrants of the vine.
The only clothing: Pantomime's white face...
His subtle smile, the inebriated vibe –
Bemused in the center of the naked ten.
Is Thalia among them? Could her voice
Animate the laughter of this sylvan tribe?

Wine! More wine! It's in the Bacchic heart
To celebrate the weekend all the week...
An edict most Olympians applaud...
The poppers pop! Fermenting in his art,
The magic moment 'party' seekers seek:
A bacchanal for Heaven's newest god!

Eduardo Gunkla Encounters Roosterman By A Stream, 1995 – 20"X 16"

XXII

EDUARDO GUNKLA ENCOUNTERS ROOSTERMAN BY A STREAM

Falling in streams of light below the stream
That's falling in streams of light into the river –
A confluence of shadow, light, and flow –
A confluence of thought, from waking dreams –
As the earth remakes its bed for the water,
That sluices quickly through the lucid shallows,

Moving as a constant, liquid in this light...
Deep in this dream we find Eduardo Gunkla –
Blended behind a tree in long brown robe –
Listening to the waters and its flight
Into the fluid forests of amnesia –
Where Roosterman scurries through his frontal lobe.

Bertie Williams: Roosterman – and the seed
Of a recurring nightcock – not nightmare –
Is moving away as though he senses someone
Is watching – but he has just been freed –
Is wary of the chains of deep despair –
The vaudeville of the shadow of the sun.

Wood Dieties In The Gully, 1995 – 17" X 15"

XXIII

WOOD DEITIES IN THE GULLY

Ravaged by shafts of light in streaming veils,
The woodland deities gather by a stream
To bathe in the lustrous warmth of Rapture's eyes.
Wherever we go – whatever light reveals –
We're in the sensual shadows of a dream...
Rays sluice through the windows of the eyes –

A pitcher of light is poured upon her skin
To make her negligee as sheer as passion...
As she lies, her pose invites disguise,
Though underneath and in – her body open –
The rivers of her are streaming through the glen –
(As all blithe spirits listen to her eyes)

Past subtle stones – translucent in the din...
The shallows of clear waters pool beside her –
Reflections that can measure waking dreams
That hear the quiet of the woods that listen
Whenever Vantage leads us into Rapture –
That is the light from which this water streams.

Waterbearers In The Woods, 2001 – 65" X 50"

XXIV

WATERBEARERS IN THE WOODS

Waterbearers walk in a ladder of light
That drops from the rock-face hidden
In shadows – striations form rungs –
The spring feeds the water, the spigot
Releases – the blue stream drops to the urn,
Shaped like the woman who kneels among

Women: to carry the vessel back to the tribe.
At the edge of the clearing, close to the ledge,
The thirsty are watching the bearers of water
Begin the procession – the deliberate climb –
Balanced and slow – as they walk the rock steps
Their chatter rewards a summer of laughter –

With all the food gathered, the clear water poured...
They bear the cool water high on their heads –
As vessels of clay and vessels of flesh –
And reflect all the light that the forest absorbed...
Tranquil and quiet, nudes in the woods,
Who move like opiates adrift in a mist.

Rupturing Poussin, 1978-82 – 72" X 54"

XXV

RUPTURING POUSSIN

Down the stream of shadows dream the vales,
As if to animate the shapes and colors
That liquefy and melt in the forest light...
The mask of the faun, the Graces – ever gentle –
The muse and poet – wading there together,
As Flora arrives – mounted on the goat –

Her thighs so thick that even Pegasus,
Steady in his gallop, in his wings,
Would fly her to forest, to the stream,
And never throw her – in her innocence –
Yet – knowing there are shadows in all things,
As goats and men are never as they seem.

She holds the pointed goat horn as a pommel –
And cocks her head – defensive with disdain –
As this is the day that eyes avoid each other,
Each distracted, rendering the subtle
Disconnect of each to each refrain:
There is this silence – this... the silencer –

Primavera, 1974-76 – 50" X 40"

XXVI

PRIMAVERA

You can never strip her of her instincts
To turn the planet's winter into spring,
To bring to life the children of the Union,
As if the eye of nature ever blinked,
As if the maiden form of everything
Never took the shape of this effusion,

Never brought the flowers and the children,
Never knew change – explosive in the womb,
Or never rode the raptor until dawn.
Primavera – master of collusion –
Mistress of the revival, of the bloom,
The pistil and the stamen: on and on...

These are the dulcet moments of renewal,
The honeysuckle sweetness on the tongue,
The flowers of love alive and green and fresh,
The lovers entwined – their feelings – magical...
And all things present, all things ever sung
Continue the fruitful dance – the spring of flesh.

Roosterboy Tormented By Woodland Deities, 2004-2014 – 49"X 33"

XXVII

ROOSTERBOY TORMENTED BY WOODLAND DEITIES

How in the beautiful woods do we find such souls
Tormenting Roosterboy below the waterfall
That pours in a liquid veil before the cave?
A curtain of light emerges and dissolves –
As though sun-showers hide where all
The fluid valence of their waters can have

The brightest of effect... The Pipes of Pan,
Played by that puckish imp, have no harmony
To offer Water, who babbles on – annoyed
By the fetching of her spirits by the hand
Of coxcombed Roosterboy – just as annoyed as she –
For naked woodland deities, temptingly deployed,

Illuming from the heartland of the linen,
One with a breast a breath-away from breath...
Distract him... Yes, Roosterboy is annoyed –
He came to bear the water not the passion –
But now he thinks to stay, until and after death
Where his 'cock-a-doodle-do' can wake the void.

The Mural Painter, 1972 – 24" x 24"

XXVIII

THE MURAL PAINTER

Below the water streams of Aqua light
Blaze in the bright reflection of the palette –
The crystal heads of whitecaps in the falls...
The manifest maker – semi-sybarite,
Looks upon himself – as though the silhouette
Of universes painted in parallels –

That dance in the cool containment of the banks,
Softened by grasses flowing to the edge –
Awaits the brush that's cleansing in the water
That he enlivens with what he does or makes,
Streams – irradiant streams – irradiate knowledge –
Shirtless in the miracle of wonder...

He stands upon the scaffold as the painter
Painting the painter painting him as he,
And brings the brilliant blues the rain of white –
The softest light – of love – an inner laughter
That brightens from his face – his reverie –
Radiant figures – dawn in the Aqua light.

William Blake And His Wife Reading 'Paradise Lost' While Nude In Their Garden, 2014 – 35" X 25"

XXIX

WILLIAM BLAKE AND HIS WIFE READING MILTON

Deep in the shadows of Urizen's hollow,
Blake and his wife – in naturalists' disguise –
Are listening to the blinding light of Milton,
Heard in the darkness of his voice's sorrow...
What is the wonder in Blake's doubting eyes?
Not every apple bedevils this temptation,

As surely there is light where there is red...
His floating wife, her hand upon his shoulder,
To ground them, to avoid the Icarian sun,
Promises fruit and manna in their bed...
Even if Milton darkens in their pleasure,
There's error in his thinking: two are one.

If God is great, she wants the apple eaten,
As everything she wants she gets or makes...
The purity of matter: flesh and bone –
Ascribed to the guilty antics of this 'Satan'.
His sentence was ordained by 'Christian' snakes,
So 'Satan as Hero' wafts through Milton's tome.

The Garden Of Eden With Sir Isaac Newton Appearing As Adam, 2014 – 50" X 42"

XXX

THE GARDEN OF EDEN WITH SIR ISAAC NEWTON APPEARING AS ADAM

While we're in the woods, let's find the garden...
God's messenger, in petticoat of lace,
Bears a fig-leaf gown for naked Eve,
Recently descended from Isaac Newton,
The gravity of reason on his face,
As is his sacred effort to believe...

Sir Isaac has travelled far beyond his limits
To calculate the tides, the sun, the stars,
Yet, wonders how this edible apple floats,
As though it is suspended by the spirits
Whose spirits square the soul of circular:
Two half-moons rise below the petticoats...

The serpent leers, suspended in the limbs,
The tree of knowledge twisted as its soul...
For 'Adam' it's the atom or the apple...
The weight of light is gravity to him...
Yet, his questions make the thunder roll –
The planets spin, the tidal currents pull...

Epistemology Of Flora, 2009 – 56" X 48"

XXXI

EPISTEMOLOGY OF FLORA

A curtain of sunlight trembles in his hands.
Apollo draws the veil so all can see
That waterfalls of light, in sheer cascades,
Nourish the sun-bright flora of this land.
In the vales of clear transparency
A lucid light envelops all the shades.

There is a certain science in the sun –
As much as there's a mystic in the rain,
As much as there is color for the bees
To bring their message to another 'one'...
And with that said, these flowers will sustain,
And permeate the colors of the trees...

She casts forget-me-nots like butterflies
That float and flutter – brilliant in light's sheen –
Like hummingbirds, they hover – Zephyr's wings –
And form a glorious garland for her eyes,
Light as the blue the red the white the green –
A bright bouquet to animate all things.

Christ And Relativity, 1970 – 24" X 21"

XXXII

CHRIST AND RELATIVITY

Outside the edge of the painting – nature
Continues its climb: what's living, what's not:
The Tree of Bodies twists upon the ledge,
As though Rilke's soul animates each figure...
The Tree of Knowledge – rooted in the serpent –
(Who disguised himself and offered privilege

Now tempts the beautiful lovers on the moss)
Aspires to rise towards the light it left...
Though God won't ask of any to repent,
For Christ is risen of and off the cross,
And floats before the vision and the art
Of mother and infant born magnificent.

What's relative is dimension and perspective
In all that is there: suspended or in motion –
Earth and air – gravity deified – the living dead –
The transparency that asks the clouds to move,
To let light stream upon the light's devotion –
And things outside to dance inside the head.

Eduardo Gunkla Dances Out OF The Woods, 1995 – 54" X 36"

XXXIII

EDUARDO GUNKLA DANCES OUT OF THE WOODS

Why not pirouette to the Pipes of Pan
When leaving one dimension for the next –
Or dance in a nimble spin upon reentry
Into the world of fields – of clearing wind?
Wind will bear us to the canals of Venice –
The softened light alive as a reverie –

The garret studio – the Venice of the Mind –
Where beautiful Flora knits lights into lace –
Eduardo dances with his model-bride –
Flora Gunkla – a vision who was divined
By a coincidence – a face to face...
Such is their love, their love is deified,

So they become the favorites of the clowns,
The water nymphs, the satyrs, the divine.
The trees who gave protection bend towards them,
Who lived and laughed among their greens and browns,
As dusk embraces memories of dawn,
As words escape the essence of their hymn.

BOOK TWO

Roosterman In The Barn, 1992 – 35" X 24"

XXXIV

ROOSTERMAN IN THE BARN

As they left the woods they saw a structure
Somewhere behind the mists that came with dusk,
The clapboards on the barn were crudely hewn,
The local hemlock – spiked with electric splinters –
That bled the fingers groping in the dark,
While eyes adjusted to the light therein...

Roosterman had travelled from the stream...
Knew that the two would see him thrice again,
And so he sat – secluded in his corner –
Windows lit with twilight just behind him...
This strange and reappearing citizen
Of a world where 'anything' is an answer –

As long as it sounds like 'light is relevant'.
'Awash in his rooster tail, his coxcomb red,
And feeling strange – we scurry to the loft...
From here we hope to fly to where we went
Before the winds, whirring through our heads,
Had us leave the window on the drafts...'

Puck And Helena: Midsummer Night's Dream, 2012 – 50" X 42"

XXXV

PUCK AND HELENA

How do they fly from hayloft to the city,
Leaving the woods, the faded clapboard barn?
Is there an airborne way from there to Venice?
They morph and float – a strange co-entity –
Puck and Helena – drifting with the dream –
That Puck may be her beloved Demetrius,

As he is the one with potion in his eyes...
So she bears her breast for her true lover –
A puckish peer – in part – or so it seems –
That she is sure... her silence steadies...
The shadows in the shaded atmosphere
Unmask the past and future – aery forms...

And what is sheer is silken in the moon
Whose light must lift them far beyond the wind
Into the silent spaces where they know
The garrets of Venice: solstice in their June...
Are coming: as they float, so they suspend –
Dreaming that all that is is coming soon...

The Fortune Teller, 1983-84 – 30" X 50"

XXXVI

THE FORTUNE TELLER

'I sense that I am seeing, so I'm silent –
Invited by the light within the ball...
The eye of the moon – aglow upon the sphere...
Like the spirits around us, we are quiet –
The mesmers of the magic protocol...
Our phosphor eyes to listen and to hear...

Through the wizard's window we have come
To see light's angels dance across your breasts...
Even as what's foretold has not been said
And as you are my smokey opium,
The hookah shares the Angels of Content...
All the knowing is breathing: we are wed...

By fortuneteller, curtains, and the light
(That moved us from the woods to ever here).
The moon is magnificent and all-expectant,
And as we find the magic-side of night
Our fortune is confirmed, our wonder – clear –
And all of time's embrace to implement.'

Venetian Window 3, 1992 – 52" X 28"

XXXVII

VENETIAN WINDOW III

'What a world we live in as we gaze
Through windows that face the northern,
Eastern light: hinged as a shutter –
The light in the lattice – the empyreal glaze –
The regal robe – its sea of purple stars –
Shadows that cross reflections that mirror

The deep dominion's dream of morning light...
Now we see before us what came after
Night's empurpled sky returned to blue...
We watch at once the vision of our night,
Fixed upon the same empyreal matter:
The mysteries and the magic of 'you'...

Whatever there is ahead is now behind –
In us the future is present and is perfect,
As is the breast that feeds the silken skein
Draped in the light that made it: the mind
Beyond all 'knowing' – the moment: consummate...
Like every instant that love has ever been.'

Lovers In Venice, 1973 – 21" X 17"

XXXVIII

LOVERS IN VENICE

'As we awoke we knew it was our window...
It was morning... it was evening... it was night...
Days were only dreams that we imagined...
Affection lit the lamp of afterglow...
What we sensed we knew – as it was perfect...
Daylight's brittle brilliance had been softened...

As my hands removed the slightest trace of silk –
It shuddered from her shoulders... through her skin –
The mirror behind us shivered in our warmth...
And as she moved her thigh I felt a spark...
I knew that a trance was on me and within
That beauty was soft and close and was our truth...

Though red may be a color of a passion,
It's still the light that makes the color red –
The blues and whites and yellows shape the tones...
The outside left outside – the inside in...
And all that was poignant leapt upon our bed...
Naked, we felt pure touch move through our zones.'

Artist And Model, 1990 – 24" X 20"

Flora At Venetian Window, 1992 – 52" X 36"

XL

THE BATH ATTENDANT

'Our Venice garret shared a common bath
In which my darling, dearest to my soul,
Washed away the sand, the woods, the hayloft,
Cleansed by all her daylight, love, and warmth,
Refreshed by the water, waiting for a towel,
With all the colors, textures – lush and soft.

Flora was not surprised to see the Prom Queen –
(She saw the rose-pink gown she'd worn to Prom) –
Arrived from the woods to attend that evening's ball...
She sat upon her purple throne to preen,
Then asked the Bath Attendant if he'd come,
And told them both: 'In fact, come one, come all...

It is the Magician's Ball... and poets, saints,
And creatures – great and small – are coming, too.
There will be mages, music – many scenes
Your lover can see, experience, and paint...'
The Bath Attendant said he'd come as Virtue –
That Beauty and Truth will come as Cajun Queens.'

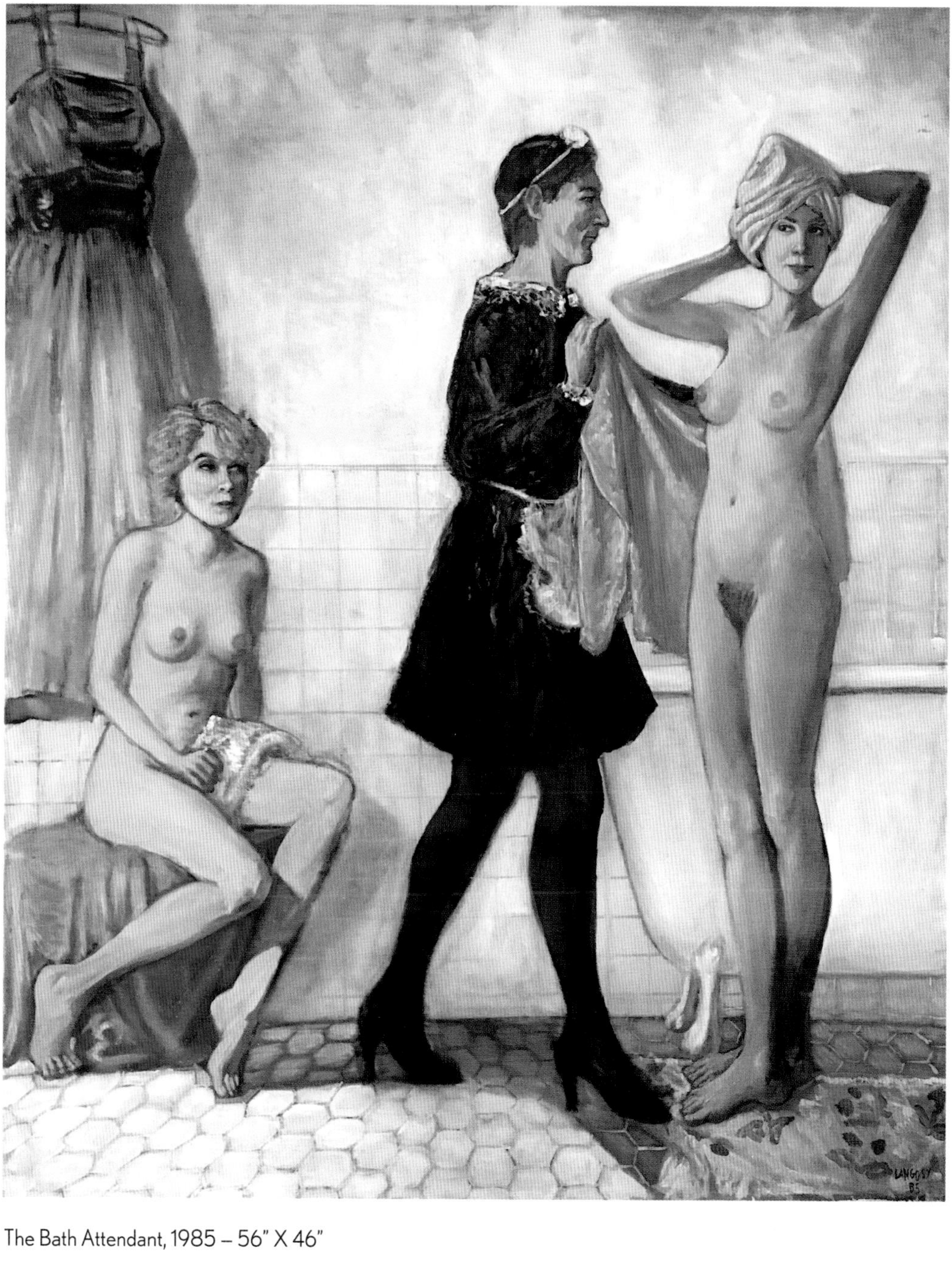

The Bath Attendant, 1985 – 56" X 46"

XXXIX

ARTIST AND MODEL

'Absorbed as I am, my Dear, in all you are,
My brush has taken hold of all my thoughts,
My fingertips tend to channel what I see...
The palette spins so quickly it's a sphere:
Mood and image are plaited by the touch,
And all that I see is 'you' and 'you and me'...

At least until the light becomes your skin –
Your skin becomes the luster in my eyes,
And I can't distinguish what I never knew
Until we appeared – before we have been –
There and back – made modest by the skies –
So the green curtains shelter us from view.

I feel your eyes and thoughts upon me now...
I know you are sensing just how gone I am...
Melded by moods – things we both divined –
I see what I feel and know in a moment how
The strength of your body is what I've become,
So now I can touch the magic of your mind.'

XLI

FLORA AND COXCOMBED MAN

'Flora, my coxcomb bustles on my head.
Let's leave this flat and dance upon the ball...
We can bounce our laser radar on the tower:
It's bats-in-the-belfry out there, it's been said...
Yet... we can leave love's room and see-it-all:
The children lost too quickly to their power,

The lost who reached too quickly for their fame,
The greedy – whose bowls are gilded to their hands –
So they can eat the bitter sweets they take...
The miracles gifted: yellow columbine –
The anklet and the vase, the crown of garlands,
The figure of your form – the fingers wake –

As if we could encircle or encompass –
(The arm upon my lap is in the eaves) –
The radiant orange washing evening skies...
Dear, you have this supple elegance –
A cherry blossom – just before the leaves –
Let's dance until we can not see our eyes.'

Clown/Bacchus Juggles Grapes Beside The Afternoon Light, 1980 – 42" X 31"

XLII

YOUNG BACCHUS JUGGLES FOR THE MODEL

'What is the love that leads us through the door
Into the world outside that I don't know...
As every effort leads me to retreat
Into the hours that pass without the clamor
Of misery and aggression? I will go –
And compromise my psyche on the street...

Perhaps, before we leave, it's time for spirits
To celebrate the space that we attend –
The sensate mind, the light's inebriation,
Our matter become the mix of elements,
Realities we are willing to suspend,
Even if here there is some infiltration

Of all the madness – so... let's pour the wine,
And tipsy-toe wherever the Laughters go –
Let's dress up – fine – so... ever as we are –
Fashion can never dress down the divine...
In our cups, I'm sure the night will follow
The night that followed the sun that followed the star.'

A Year In My Life, 1984 – 50" X 32"

XLIII

ARTIST AND MODEL: DRESSING FOR THE MAGICIAN'S BALL

'I'm always comfortable within your skin –
Although your outfit seems a bit risqué,
If you wear it – you will cause a stir –
That shakes the tree, the apples of our Eden,
Delicious on our lips, that fruitful day...
And what if – if your wings are gossamer –

Molded from the sheerest cloth you wear,
Could you then assemble – in my mind –
The form of you projected everywhere?
And what if – if your shadows could appear
Within yourself, the shadow-self entwined
With crimson colors – woven in the air –

Until the light upon you changes tones,
Could you become the shadow and its form?
I am the one – your escort into light –
A loose-fit jacket made of monotones –
To balance your brilliance – utterly conform –
It's madness that will witness us tonight!'

Santa Maria Della Salute, 1977 – 21" X 20"

XLIV

SANTA MARIA DELLA SALUTE HOSTS THE BALL

The water lay at the feet of flights of stairs,
As we approached the Palace of the Ball –
The evening gilded on the rising steps
Into the great Rotunda of the Airs...
We could not hear a footfall – not at all –
Nor could we find a way to be adept

When dancing with the lithe and winged things
That began to assemble, chanting to the Arc,
To open her gates and let the Trojans in...
The Heavens reign forever in this singing,
The echoes of the saints in all the music,
The fervor of the pitch upon the wind...

We stand on the piazza, while the gates
Open to let the gathered throng pass through
And bounce their raucous voices off the dome,
Then – into the quiet chapels... there are eight...
And then, of course, there is the 'One of You',
That I will call 'The Chapel of Our Home'...

Carnival Of Chaos, 1973-86 – 71" X 67"

XLV

CARNIVAL OF CHAOS: HIGH WIRE IN THE ROTUNDA OF SANTA MARIA DELLA SALUTE

How can you 'walk a tightrope' with no string,
Or dance on a light beam – unseen by the throng?
I'm balanced upon a ferris wheel of light –
The vision of you before me – on your swing –
O – how can one ever sing if there's no song?
The Angels add the slightest bit of weight

To spin the wheel while I stand and stare
At constellations: Color's flesh and bone –
The clamoring crowd in festivals of silk –
The fireworks of the Khan upon the air –
Ambient flame that saturates the tone –
The powder-keg just waiting for the spark!

The anarchy of space – contained in time –
The distance of a breath until its next...
The breathless way I stand in front of you –
All these fancies balanced in my mind...
That, if it was not clear, would be annexed –
By visionless prophets – windowless of view...

The All-Around Maid, 1985 – 56" X 46"

XLVI

THE BATH ATTENDANT, MASQUERADING AS THE ALL-ROUND MAID, CONFESSES IN THE CHAPEL OF THE BATH OF SANTA MARIA DELLA SALUTE

So good to be the dresser of the Graces,
As I have found a way to fit the form,
That would have been a brutish monotone,
But I have been a man of many faces,
And I have worn their tattoos on my arm,
And I can make a flower of a stone

And I can choose what you can choose, so I
Know the 'male' and 'female' and am one –
As both are balanced in this cloth of skin...
I spoke with Blake, I spoke with Keats, and I
Am fluid in the faith – I hold the sun,
And melt before the powers that are within...

Prince has left his costumes for the Ball...
I know the Graces favored what he wore,
Exquisite silks and satins: loose and free –
The diamond stilts, the brilliant crystal heels,
The costumes in my closest are a door –
And what I am is what I'm meant to be.

Bacchus Surprises Three Young Graces At Their Toilette , 1985 – 24" x 20"

XLVII

YOUNG BACCHUS AND THE THREE GRACES – SURPRISE IN THE BOUDOIR OF THE CHAPEL OF THE BATH OF SANTA MARIA DELLA SALUTE

Pulcinella's feelin' kinda freaky –
back – behind the mask – behind the eyes...
dressed in white: a venal masquerade,
the agent of the Graces getting jiggy...
pimped-out in immaculate disguise
to welcome and invite a rich parade

of deviants, fiends, and friends, as long as they
bring the coins that pay for shoes and hats,
that pay for caviar and drop-top whips,
to put his fancy folly on display
in front of all the drunken celebrants,
who drink their heady cups with un-kissed lips.

Love can not be bought – but can be sold...
the mission: to emancipate and dance
with Zeus' daughters... He will understand
Young Bacchus brings the flowers – not the gold –
garlands in his hair to help his balance,
a bouquet in his grip to hide his hand.

The Prom Queen, 1983 – 50" X 30"

XLVIII

THE PROM QUEEN: ONE LEG UP IN THE CHAPEL OF HIGH FASHION OF SANTA MARIA DELLA SALUTE

The castanets are waiting in the wings –
Caustic consonants that click clack click...
Fingertips that snap the cymbal shells,
Bells within the ears that ring ring ring,
Legs that notch the hip, the thighs so thick,
The body of a dancer – quick-flex-muscle,

Shoulders poised to twist upon her core...
Lithe as a leopard – feline in her grace –
Tight, yet supple chest – her lifted breasts...
From top to toe, agile lines... that taper! –
A consequential moment on her face,
Adrenaline-aware, the click clack castanets

Tremble in the rhythms that she siphons –
Pent-up motion in her necklaced neck...
One leg flesh – and one leg – waterfalls
Of fashion-forward, violet-pink chiffons,
That swish swish swish to the click clack click...
The Prom Queen – Queen Flamenco – of the ball...

American Vaudeville, 1983 – 39" X 26"

XLIX

AMERICAN VAUDEVILLE: IN THE CHAPEL OF COMMEDIA DELL'ARTE OF SANTA MARIA DELLA SALUTE

In the midst of Vaudeville – these theatrics –
Emerson in the role of Roosterman,
Thoreau the bard, the ever wistful thought
Hung upon the branch of non-specifics –
The sea that is as equal as the land.
The scene is staged upon a curtained set...

Eva Tanguay is singing: 'I Don't Want It' –
Not nothing nowhere never – if at all...
Her vocals are dismissive of perfection,
Her stage forgotten as the sun that set...
The poignance of the scene is gestural...
The passing of a time – the hand's inflection

Seems to speak of silence wired for sound...
But I must paint the tangible in fact,
Even if just light lounging on the chaise,
That intimates the shape that it surrounds,
As thought and light commingle in the act
That watches you – indifferent to praise.

115

The Marriage Of Don Diego de Acedo (the king's signet bearer) To The Infanta Margarita Seranaded By The Great Comic Opera Singer Manelli, With Fireworks, As A Homage to Velázquez, 1974-83 – 45" X 41"

L

THE MARRIAGE OF DON DIEGO TO THE INFANTA SERENADED BY MANELLI: IN THE (RECENTLY NAMED) ACCA-CHAPELLO OF FIGARO OF SANTA MARIA DELLA SALUTE

The Carnival of Chaos wears the colors
Of fireworks now emblazoned in his suit –
Just beyond the curtain of the Chapel...
The Marian Muse unveils the gossamer
Nightgown of a wedding dress – invites,
To her peaceful virgin citadel,

Groomsman Don Diego – geniusly gallant –
As if the subtle shadows of his eyes
Watch us watching what he is reflecting –
The shadowless eyes of Beauty's debutante.
Perfection has no need to compromise...
And She is listening to Manelli's singing,

While Don Diego's dwarf prepares the wine,
With every portal as open as her ears,
To welcome her husband to their lovers' bed –
Like poor Pierrot, enrapt with Columbine.
The ageless is inclusive of all years –
Their children's children's children watch them wed.

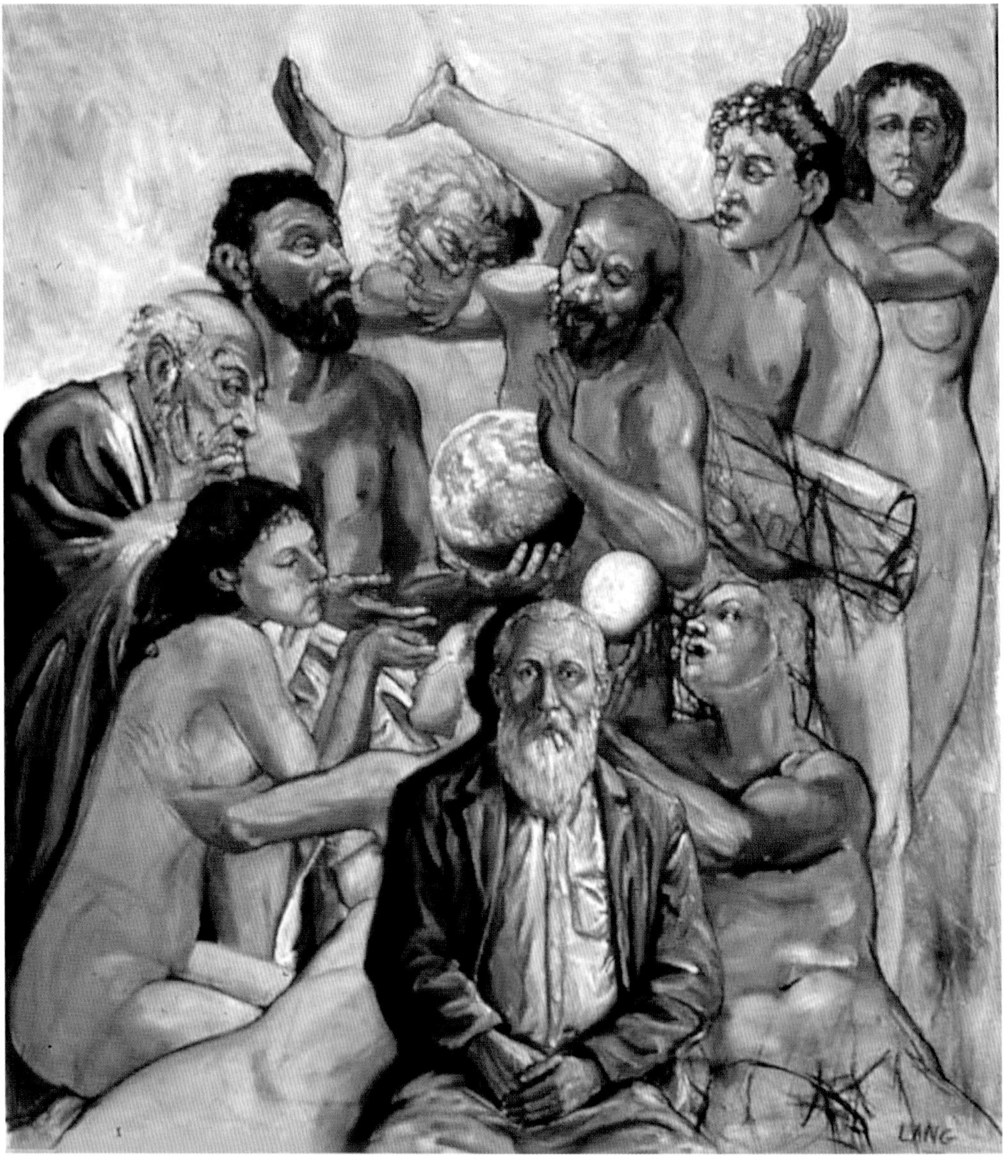

The Mural Painter, 1976 – approx. 42" x 40"

LI

THE MURAL PAINTER: IN THE CHAPEL OF THE VISION OF INQUIRIES OF SANTA MARIA DELLA SALUTE

If Atlas holds the globe upon his fingers
And balances the moonlight with the sun,
Then as the gods assemble in his thoughts –
Soon to move as ideas into figures –
And find perspective in the love of one,
Whose mythic body is breathing light

Into the eyes that train upon the ceiling,
To see these gods and Angels from a stage,
A scaffold to paint the feather-weight of light –
A citadel to hear the prophets singing –
That, as an expression, illustrates the age...
Now we seek the shelter of our thoughts

In chapels of the ageless – sun and stars –
Apollo and Atlas, Selene and Zeus –
Forms that are not with us though we feel them –
As if the Venus-passion lies in Mars,
As if the Martian power lies in Venus,
As if the brush strokes wait upon the forms.

Greed Receiving The Head Of Pierrot, 1985 – 60" X 48"

LII

GREED RECEIVING THE HEAD OF PIERROT IN THE CHAPEL OF PLAYFUL TORMENT AND DEATH OF SANTA MARIA DELLA SALUTE

Greed is an old blind fool with a selfish heart –
If only a heart by name if not in fact –
At his feet the bodies of jewels are strewn...
Around his wrists the golden coils of serpents...
Fingers like rakes, the counts to be exact,
A bracelet of silver pearls dripped from the moon,

Eyes fixed upon the nothingness of things,
Miserable baubles signifying nothing,
Accumulating riches with no end –
His craven appetite manipulating...
Every thought connected to the strings
Of power: to increase the dividend,

Or rape and take, murder and defile,
Sick with lust for diamonds, peridots,
For sapphires, rubies, the blood of olivine...
His gilded skin – his burnished, tarnished soul
Receives the painted head of dead Pierrot,
And craves the tragic comic's Columbine...

Taking Of A Soul, 2008 – 56" X 48"

LIII

TAKING OF A SOUL IN THE CHAPEL OF PLAYFUL TORMENT AND DEATH OF SANTA MARIA DELLA SALUTE

As often as not the hero is the goat,
The tales of selfless sacrifice are mute,
The gut is opened by the prelate's knife,
The soul suspended as the body floats,
And what is sacred has become a brute –
Bleeding the tepid fluids of a life

That has been defiled by hope and prayers
That sped good wishes to the hearts of others,
Leaving the gullet open for abuse –
The terrible torments of the heartless fire.
Beneath the wings of angels and the mother
Who has no time for the son who has no use,

He drips his waning blood upon the back
Of one who loved him – now in another's arms,
While the life of him – the good who loved –
Is under the knife – the spiritual attack –
Of terror and despair – and death's alarums...
The things of men that are not the things of God...

The Temptormation Of St. Antonio, 2014 – 37" X 36"

LIV

THE TEMPTORMATION OF SAINT ANTONIO IN THE CHAPEL OF PLAYFUL TORMENT AND DEATH OF SANTA MARIA DELLA SALUTE

Saint Antonio sits upon the dais
And watches as terrible horrors drift on by;
His consciousness unclouded by the terror,
And yet he feels the anguish of remorse,
As all the torments bugle in his eye...
The malevolent harpy – screeching in his ear –

Lashes her serpent tongue upon his brain,
The wizard ghoul, with talon to plug the sound,
Inserted in ear so lashings cannot escape,
Makes bats to drive the belfried saint insane...
The submarine-breasted headdress – fatly cheeked –
Drips her venomous serum on his nape,

While miserable demon lunches on his arm,
And phantom male, with childless female breasts,
Would feed his hungry lips a bloody bowl
Of all the Temptormation's poisoned charms...
Ah – but this grotesqueness is a test –
And Saint Antonio seeks to save his soul.

The Misplaced Tenor, 2009 – 30" X 25"

LV

THE DISPLACED SOPRANO IN THE CHAPEL OF THE ECHO OF LOST SONG OF SANTA MARIA DELLA SALUTE

Having never heard the Viking song,
Nor sung of braided blondes, of fattened breasts,
Fed by the milk of oxen – succulence...
But – Manelli is singing loudly to a throng
Of Histories that vanished in the conquest
Of Empires that had lost their innocence,

And with it lost their heart-sung, ruptured sagas,
As decadence and greed had made them fat,
Indolent of spirit, and fodder for the sword,
The vengeance of the changing of the eras,
The swift disposal of the ignorant,
The malice in the anger of a word...

She wears the helmet of the sons of Odin,
Now poisoned by the arrow of Amor...
Her belly pierced – the clashing of the ages –
The eagle wings, the helmet of the Roman...
Thus the soprano's duet with the tenor
Sings of change – and all that it displaces.

Roosterman In St. Peter's Chair, 1979-84 – 40" X 30"

LVI

ROOSTERMAN IN SAINT PETER'S CHAIR IN THE CHAPEL OF THE COCK OF SANTA MARIA DELLA SALUTE

The Monsignor in the mirror holds his rod
To strike the one forlorn, who sits in sadness –
The innocent clown lit by the feather of fire –
While Roosterman contemplates an act of God,
Presented by the prelate to his highness,
An inquisition as to what is higher:

To strike an innocent – or pardon a fool...
The bristling cock rushes through the window,
And Judas cowers, knowing his hour comes...
As Roosterman sits below upon God's stool,
Not throne, not chair, the lowest of the low,
And seeks to find an otherworldly kingdom...

This is the perfect time for meditation –
To never speak again of love as love,
To understand the nature of the perverse,
And find in nothingness a revelation –
That everything around us is depraved...
That this is the truth that rules the universe.

Original Sin, 2000 – 68" X 56"

LVII

ORIGINAL SIN IN THE CHAPEL OF THE VISION OF INQUIRIES OF SANTA MARIA DELLA SALUTE

'Adam has fallen... so has he arisen...
At this time, as a she, or so it seems...
Venus attends her birth upon the sea –
The cross is nailed together in a vision –
A symbol of the punishment of dreams
That would lift the 'self' beyond the 'me'...

As though we were evil or are evil still...
His lover chose to nourish him with fruit...
Forever chastened and misunderstood,
As her intentions – innocent of her will –
Gave him a gift she nourished in her heart –
Never has evil ever done such good...

'Original sin' invents us as we are...
And – as I am no judge, I sit and watch
The central figure – in her holy trance –
As modest as a cloud before a star –
As she prepares the waters that will quench
The child who so reveres her *sustenance*.'

Crucifixion In The Time Of, 2000 – 42" X 30"

LVIII

CRUCIFIXION IN THE TIME OF... IN THE CHAPEL OF THE VISION OF INQUIRIES OF SANTA MARIA DELLA SALUTE

Before I found X I fled from Ra,
Somewhere in the desert of the sea...
In this – the third dimension of robotics –
Muscles of war destroy my Shangri-La,
And I know not if God is my enemy,
Or if this question asks the heretics

If whatever truth they know can crucify
The atoms of dust that obviate the sands,
So that they cut the eyes until they bleed
Before the reason ever asked the why,
Or before I put my life into your hands,
Not knowing if the wind would bend the reed...

Oh God what have I done? What have you made?
This wooden cross unanchored and adrift...
I do not doubt I doubt, but ask for you
To signify me – even as I fade
Back into the eras from which I lift...
My body as bread, my blood as manna dew.

Christ Bearing His Cross, 2000 – 32" X 25"

LIX

CHRIST BEARING HIS CROSS IN THE CHAPEL OF THE VISION OF INQUIRIES OF SANTA MARIA DELLA SALUTE

Pierrot is on the backside of the Cross
Being borne by the son who has no father,
Whose mother was made a virgin by the fact.
Before there is a birth there is a loss,
And what if there is another – then another –
The ages and their continuum intact...

A constant crucifixion – suffered pain –
Bearing the weight of others – even clowns.
The coxcombed Roman-togaed Roosterman,
Appears in the strangest quadrants of the Brain,
Bearing his sword – a witness to the sounds
Of anguish... The mother's tear-stained hands

Hide her eyes from the agony and despair,
Hope dispelled by the cycle of persecution
That seeks to divide the tribes and separate
Man from God, the desert from the air,
All for the sake of some vile institution,
That seeks to control – not to liberate...

The Crucifixion Of The Father And The Son, 2014 – 42" X 24"

LX

THE CRUCIFIXION OF THE FATHER AND THE SON IN THE CHAPEL OF THE VISION OF INQUIRIES OF SANTA MARIA DELLA SALUTE

The father is dying. Who will watch the son?
The death of God is in the heartless air.
The prelate and the soldier have no feelings.
While Mary sobs upon the shroud of Turin,
The broken feet she kisses in despair
Cannot support the weight of any teachings

Other than death is final – God has died –
At least for those whose faith defies belief
That life itself is sacred and is one,
By all the murders they have sanctified:
The precedents of shock and awe, the grief –
As greed and power monopolize the sun.

'But here there is no light'* – perhaps a question –
A brazen portrait shouldered by a man
Who cannot understand the fate of art,
How coxcombed Peter appears as Roosterman,
Why death becomes a monument of reason,
And crucifies the son, and kills the heart.

*Keats, 'Ode to a Nightingale'

The Descent Of Charlie, 1978-83 – 43" X 33"

LXI

THE DESCENT OF CHARLIE IN THE CHAPEL OF THE VISION OF INQUIRIES OF SANTA MARIA DELLA SALUTE

Think what you will of pagans or of saints –
The gentle have been encrimsoned by the fire –
The low glow of the moon – the candle flame –
Candescing in the pulses of the paints –
The misty light of shadows in a gyre –
The light of love that no one can profane –

Lies in the sacrificial bones of Charlie –
All the characters of life have gathered –
In wrapt remorse – in shock and disbelief –
The testament anew – the tragedy –
The beings that have suffered – tarred and feathered –
Are witness to this cataclysmic grief –

The little tramp – defiled – descends the tree –
The life was taken from him – then the earth
Gave his body back for more derision –
The hatred – greed – the pomp of jealousy –
And if there is a meaning to his birth –
It is his death – from which he has arisen –

Apotheosis Of Pulcinella, 1982 – 84" X 71"

LXII

APOTHEOSIS OF PULCINELLA IN THE CHAPEL OF CLOUDS OF SANTA MARIA DELLA SALUTE

The flight of angels lifted him with wings –
Feathers made of wind and light and clouds –
That shoulder blades had sprouted in the flight
Into the aery atmosphere – into the whirring
Spaces – where worlds above below surround
Unmeasured tones in veils of sheer delight –

Effusive laughter – bright as children's eyes –
Warm as the naked flesh that feels the love –
Sentient moments – held by arms and hands...
'Only the good are merry', say the skies,
Embracing Pulcinella – dressed like a dove –
White on white – the clouds of sunlit sands,

Or sea foam in the breath of wind and air
That seat the etheric beings – there to see
The humble clown's unhuman transformation
Into the spirit of 'gods are everywhere' –
The bright transcendence of theosophy...
The changeling clown now master of the sun.

The White Clown, 1982 – 18" X 22"

LXIII

THE WHITE CLOWN: IN THE ANTECHAMBER OF THE AFTERMATH OF THE MAGICIAN'S BALL OF SANTA MARIA DELLA SALUTE

I've seen the taunts, the sleepless arrogance,
The nights that measure days in dreams of fools,
The errant passage, tiers of decadence,
The masquerade unmasked, the mezmer's glance,
The love that leaves the lover for the jewels,
The night so long – the hours of impotence –

The chapels in the towers of romance
Where prayer hides from hope and every thought
Lies exhausted, twisted, visionless –
And I could leave my life to happenstance,
Or shield my eyes to capture what I caught –
The terrible gist of genius, or of madness...

The clown's true color lighting – from behind –
All of the chaos clamoring near me –
Yet... if I'd look outside... I'd see you here –
The paint, the brush, the easel, you – my bride...
The linen stares – a blank apology –
Blinded by what I've seen – it is too clear...

Elizabeth Seated In Front Of Night Window, 1984 – 34" X 26"

LXIV

ELIZABETH SEATED IN FRONT OF NIGHT WINDOW: AFTER THE MAGICIAN'S BALL IN THE CHAPEL OF OUR HOME

Take me home my dear, yes, take me home,
Where only your love can move me to myself,
And in you I can find what you have found...
I do not know the reason you have come...
I am amazed how you've restored my health
In ways that can't be measured – so profound –

Your sensual elegance that is for me
A grounding – a reality of touch –
Soon to thrill my skin – magical affection –
A love that stirs the tides that move the sea...
How can I ever love you half as much
As you have loved me – darling of perfection?

The city night retreats before your luster,
The moonlight knows no object but your skin –
My eyes can just believe how sensual
Your nightgown is, descending from your shoulder,
How what is shown outside is shown within –
My darling, dear, my one – you're beauty-full.

An Intimate Moment Observed, 1986 – 24" X 20"

LXV

AN INTIMATE MOMENT OBSERVED

Back – before the door – inside the mirror –
The Prom Queen looks upon herself and sees
Her night is changing as it now is challenged –
Another love lies with her heart's amor,
And to her eyes the bouquet's vanities
Are blind to the perfection she alleged...

Beauty has a heartless ambiance
When wrapt in selfish wonderment of self,
Knowing that power makes a lover doubt,
She plays upon the chords of innocence,
Places the book of life back on the shelf,
And blows the candle's fire forever out.

And they no longer see, no longer hear her –
Emotions are as mutable as flesh –
She stands and stares alone – supremely lost,
Not knowing if she should leave, if she should enter,
Vengeance now the answer to her distress –
It's her own heart that she has double-crossed.

Spring Comes In Like A Clown, 1979 – 8" X 6"

LXVI

SPRING COMES IN LIKE A CLOWN IN THE CHAPEL OF OUR HOME

Through the window, while looking at the glass,
Having stared the winter through icy scenes,
Pantaloon comes – springing through the air...
My love has clasped her hands behind her – shh –
To see if her breasts are budding, like the greens,
That come with the sun and thicken everywhere –

The grass, the hedges, bushes and the trees,
The colors that change the palette and the mind,
That may have wandered like Milton in the dark,
Bearing his blackened lantern – now the breeze
Promises the warmth I had hoped to find
With missives sent in curious remarkable

Like: 'where are you, my love, it's cold outside...
The woolens, thermals, blankets, and the heat
Are here for you... let's nestle – and survive.'
Whatever the darkness I had held inside
Is floating through – the winter is complete –
And springtime brings the summer – we're alive!

BOOK THREE

Artist And Model - Red, 1984 – 24" X 16"

LXVII

ARTIST AND MODEL: REDROOM

Red is a diamond different than the others –
Its blush is deepened and its depth defines –
Ruddy fires of flambeaux flick the shadows –
The paradox is: live or love the lovers –
Even if the brush incarnadines
The amber in the measures of afterglow...

Music of light is streaming through the arches –
Morning or twilight dreaming on the flesh –
The touch of love – an ember of distraction –
Is what can move the heart through silences,
Moments when words are useless as a wish
Made before an answer, or a reason...

Only the question – quiet and composed –
Is known to either, before the red turns gold...
The brilliant yet subtle changes in the mood,
The fires that gild the passages supposed
To be the underpainting of times untold
By flesh or fire or passion – or light's blood.

Into The Room Of Dreams, 1987 – 40" X 48"

LXVIII

INTO THE ROOM OF DREAMS

Sleepless, I must lie awake and dream
Of movements in the shape of shifting forms
Of night-times that sift through the doors of day...
The light in atoms drifts in seams and seems
As lace or patterns draped upon the arms
Of all the angels that come and go away,

Or turn their backs to watch the fire of night,
Flushed in flares of flames in streaks of red,
As their ephemeral flesh is so alive
I see it in the eyes like ghosts of light –
Transparencies that dance inside my head
Like all the fathomless phantoms of my love...

Into the room of dreams I found my heart –
She had opened the light that night had closed,
And in her eyes I saw her passion move,
And with her feet I felt her touch my feet,
And startle me with all that I supposed
Would be the moment dreams would turn to love.

The Orange Room, 1984 – 48" X 38"

LXIX

THE ORANGE ROOM

Sleepless still before night's blue-black curtain –
Draped upon the wall – the orange wall –
And night's gown – still in motion on your body
With bells of stars – the music on your skin
That wakes the watching eyes that cover all
The restless minutes of your energy...

Hours that move as hours – as endless hours –
That are as ours alone – are in your hands...
My chin and cheek are comforted by touch...
Your palm and fingers simmer with a power
That moves my body – as it understands
That you and you alone I love so much...

Now in your eyes so deep I see the sun
And all the spirit shadows of your gaze
Are light as light that enters through the door
That is the window of the only one –
Who is the mirror of the hour-less days –
The orange-black, the cycles we explore.

In Celebration Of Elizabeth Turning Fifty, 2000 – 40" X 32"

LXX

IN CELEBRATION OF ELIZABETH TURNING FIFTY

Were I to see time vanish as it was,
Transparent as the flesh that once I felt,
Poured by touch into the hand I hold,
Then the constant changes as it is,
And time and place are merely what I dreamt –
Continuums that fold and then unfold...

How is it that your body is as I am –
Youthful as the age of which I dream,
And still remains, untouched by hands of time,
Provoked to paint a wonder's dithyramb,
With you the subject, essence, and the theme,
The circle round the night and candle flame,

The moments that no minutes dissipate,
The minutes that no seconds ever measure?
These fluid curtains are drawn to welcome day
Into the nights that mornings radiate...
What we left 'behind' – our present pleasure...
Tomorrow's past is timeless from today...

The Fortune Teller, 2000 – 27" X 18"

LXXI

THE FORTUNE TELLER II

I filled the crystal sphere with silvered light:
The white light fell like cumulus from the moon,
And washed the stars to help the night sky see.
My eyes became the focus – thus resplendent,
Like all the shimmers – in and out the room –
Of you and you again – you endlessly...

When do we begin to see the future
If what has been passed between us now is gone
Into a filagree we laced together –
Passages of the worlds that we inured
To settle in the seance of our song,
The silent one – the one known to each other –

That few can glimpse – unless we help them see –
A silken robe now open to undress,
A skein of skin so pale – these shadows see
Good fortune is our future – one as 'we' –
A testament – and as such I express:
I bear the crystal light you bear for me.

Muse Becomes Poet, 1984 – 50" X 40"

LXXII

MUSE BECOMES POET

The muse flew through the window all in gold –
A certain renascence upon her mind...
The rush of ages gone – and yet – undead...
And watched her self into her self unfold,
Into the voice that she had left behind –
A gilded helmet smelted on her head,

As though a life-mask poured a golden age
Through her neck and shoulders to her breast,
Down into her torso and her hips,
Until pure life – like Galatea's Mage –
Was lit by light that darkness had suppressed –
Those academics glaring at her lips,

Pursed in serious witness of the awe,
Empurpled in her dignifying robes –
The naked transformation – into vision –
The power of truth and beauty in her law...
And she – the humble conduit – the scribe –
Watched the stylus write what had been written.

Passage Of The Muse, 1976 – 35" X 28"

LXXIII

PASSAGE OF THE MUSE

Outside the window flares ignite in flames,
Yet here inside the awe is never still –
Marooned as I am by time and gravity,
In a listless age without a name,
I listened and I heard the tempest's will,
And suffered the chorus of inanity,

But then I met a poet and I knew,
That there would be a monument to song
Such as I had never heard nor sung,
And so I spent my self and as I flew
Into the hours of days that don't belong
Anywhere in time – we both grew strong...

I saw his heart and knew what we would do:
Make a passage beyond the will of those
Who seek to suffer ignorance and fear,
And wake the humble seer and reconstrue
The measures that Aristotelians chose,
That Shakespeare sang into young Keats' ear.

The Herm Of The Poet, 1994 – 72" X 52"

LXXIV

THE HERM OF THE POETS

As we ventured back into the forests
That were as shadows of our other selves,
As we moved in daylight as mere specters,
Hiding in masks so no one would suspect
The observations hidden in that stealth
Could serve as witness and as silencers

Of lethal meanings hidden in fiery words,
The criss-crossed shafts of anger and of hate,
From bludgeoning bullies full of pompous rants,
We came into the Hollow of the Absurd,
Put aside our mantle of self-debate,
Touched the Herm that pointed to the poets,

Who wrote of sensual ecstasies and God,
In the luxuriant shadows of the light,
That streamed from the various tomes of Deity,
The universal passages that laud
The tender loves, the merciful delight,
That trumps the visceral hatred that we see.

Erumpens Fecundat, 1993 – 65" X 43"

LXXV

ERUMPENS FECUNDAT

Friar Antonio queries with his quill
Before the candelabra – barely lit,
An insufficient, antique source of light…
Behind his back-brain fires are magical,
Vesuvian outbursts utter and transcendent,
Flurries of intellect the flames excite…

So Dante lies – beheaded on the table –
An inspiration dormant and severe…
Platonic – in the caverns of desire –
Friar Antonio dreams of Aristotle,
The light through the forest – like a chandelier –
And Shakespeare – just an element of fire…

How to write the meditation breaking
Upon the moment never yet unknown,
Despite the dusty volumes in the mind?
His words become a metamorphic being –
A seed that bursts into the matter sewn
Into the light the darkness has divined.

Table Tipping With St. Paul, 2014 – 37" X 36"

LXXVI

AFTER THE TEMPTORMATION, FRIAR ANTONIO SEARCHES FOR SAINT PAUL AND FINDS THE HERMIT IN HIS DESERT CAVE

Having survived his wicked Temptormation,
Friar Antonio wandered – in his frock –
Into the desert, thirsting for the hermit,
The one who left the world to find salvation
In his hidden cave carved in the rock,
Neither to live in fear nor preach from pulpit,

But rather to 'tip-the-table' with the master
And summon the spirits issued from above,
Who spoke the word issued from megaphone
Held by Poet Peter, transformed from Red Rooster,
While French Maids bear the gifts of risen loaves –
Warm baguettes, fresh-baked in High Heaven,

Which all true prophets willingly accept
Is home to the immortal and only One,
As from this power their words become prophetic,
Which only the unholy may suspect
Is from another source – or derivation...
The face of God agape upon the rock.

Blind Milton Composes *Paradise Lost* In His Mind, 2014 – 34" X 22"

LXXVII

BLIND MILTON DICTATING PARADISE LOST TO HIS DAUGHTERS

Forever now the servants of the Muse:
Those who serve him and he himself who serves –
Intolerable as the sentence of starless night –
This grave affair his children did not choose,
But, blinded by the darkness of his nerves,
Fearing the holy song would leave the light

Deep in the fiery blackness of his soul,
They felt the simple anguish of his pain,
And knew that they would have to help him pen
Words that came in dreams – so he could control
The torments that were Satan in his brain,
The rhythms and meters of his brilliant vision.

The hand of God lay close to the serpent's maw,
That smiled through brittle teeth upon the page...
Without the holy writ there was no song...
The offered apple tempted what he saw –
Aware that human error could not assuage
Satan nor God – that evil must belong.

Two Poets Meet In A Garden At Night And Then Go On Their Separate Ways, 2011 – 42"X 33"

LXXVIII

TWO POETS MEET IN A GARDEN AT NIGHT AND THEN GO ON THEIR SEPARATE WAYS

We thought we knew each other and we did,
But that was just a time a time ago...
The garden at night was fragrant, beautiful...
That we should meet this way was not intended,
Although it's true that we could never know
If other intentions made inevitable

This passage or this passing in the dark.
The night herself was lit by many objects
That were at once reflected in the motion
As things outside our eyes – and our remarks
Were cordial, as we understood the subject
Was never more important than the notion

That two who were as one could never be
As perfect as those harmonies of silence,
When quiet stops to listen to the wind,
That all the night the blind would never see
The meaning of their sole magnificence –
And so we parted... each to each... a friend...

Abduction Of The Muse, 1977-80 – 40" X 33"

LXXIX

ABDUCTION OF THE MUSE

He sat beside a table before the sea –
A feather-quill to fill the vacant page
With words that would become his legacy,
But then the demon of 'reality'
Saw his chance to steal her from the age,
And leave the poet void of poesy,

And so – with a fiery rush that swept the sky –
An arrogance that chose to test the sun,
To see whose flame would permeate the air,
He flew on his demon wings and lifted high
The sensual beauty of his inspiration,
And left him the purgatory of despair...

But no one knew that this was just a passage,
Nor that the poet would keep the feather-quill,
And hide it up his sleeve and by his heart,
Until the time would come to fill the page
With all he'd seen and heard and learned – until
The Muse returned to grace his craft and art.

A Displaced Soprano With Oratorical Poetica And A Mendicant Singer, 2016 – 42" X 40"

LXXX

A DISPLACED SOPRANO WITH ORATORICAL POETICA AND A MENDICANT SINGER

'Apollo sings in the window of the sun –
Never named – but the Father of the Muses...
The vague historians never knew the truth,
And if I remember, Mnemosyne was young,
And much too bright for Zeus and his abuses –
She loved the God of Light – eternal youth!'

So sang the Son of the Sun in bass cascades –
The oratorical waves that rocked the stage
And shook the foundations of the well-endowed,
The grim inscriptions of the world's charades,
That were the chaos of a discordant age,
Then – up leapt the mendicant singer from the crowd!

He laid the head of Zeus at the feet of her,
Who hit the highest notes in this strange quartet
Sung by these four aspirants of Pure Light...
Into the blues-reds-whites of the echo chamber –
Reverberant notes of the new Magnificat!
Vibrant voice in the ever-orange night!

Euhemerus' 'Ism' Is Interrupted, 2016 – 42" X 40"

LXXXI

EUHEMERUS 'ISM' IS INTERRUPTED BY A REPLACED POET AND A DISPLACED SOPRANO

Because I can not think to write the truth,
I might as well 'replace' the facts with nonsense,
And see if I can suffer it because
Truth itself is just the fruit of myth,
And disbelief has lost its innocence,
Suspended in the talons of its jaws...

But then, and now, my thought is interrupted
By some white bird thats seeks to snatch away
The muse who once appeared as the Soprano –
Displaced within an epic so corrupted
That there is nothing left to sing or say,
No operatic speech in her libretto,

No story-line, no archetype, no myth –
Only a dull equation sans solution,
A song without a song, without a note,
But then, my feather-quill awoke the truth,
And stopped the winged thing and the abduction
Of every note that singing Homer wrote.

Dante And Virgil, 1979 – 26" X 21"

LXXXII

DANTE AND VIRGIL

Virgil saw this Beauty in a vision,
And heard her calling in his dream of death,
Midway in the afterlife of nothing –
This quintessential essence of a pagan
Unable to divine the heavenly breadth –
According to the Christian view of being...

But, as a transcendent in the middle age,
Before the Dark Ages settled in again,
With all its despots, racists, genocides,
He rose with hope – a universal knowledge –
That love is the purest breath of oxygen –
So he and Dante – now the artist's guide –

Could see this Beauty levitate and point
Towards a realm where no one yet had gone –
And let the artist know that 'Paradise'
May only be immaculate intent –
That he may see the miracle of vision,
And trust the love in Beauty's dreaming eyes.

Ingres Serenades The Memory Of His Dead Wife's Youth, 2014 – 36"X 30"

LXXXIII

INGRES SERENADES THE MEMORY OF HIS DEAD WIFE'S YOUTH

There is a then and now that always is
A passage both before and after time...
It seems the strings might vibrate with a note...
The moments when he barely knew what was...
The music of a bell without a chime...
The loss for which there is no antidote...

The melancholy minutes of a death
That died before the body knew it gone...
The intricate fingers fashioning a wave
That rides until the end of vibrant youth...
Until the moon is swallowed by the sun
And dreams retain the memory of love...

The interludes of laughter that are sung
In the hollow shadows of the body...
The fingers that move lightly on the neck...
The serenade of strings so tightly strung...
The bridge of joy across the depths of Lethe...
The tears from which there is no turning back...

Sailing To Prospero's Isle, 2012 – 38"X 40"

LXXXIV

SAILING TO PROSPERO'S ISLE

Somewhere in the streams of light an island
Appears as an illusion made of clouds –
My child has set the rudder on her heart –
Whether or not the sea becomes the land,
Or if the sail of light is aether's shroud,
The journey can not begin before it starts,

So off we sail – into the nether aether –
The underworld of winds that move the tides,
Upon the shiftless rhythms of the sea,
So that we may become one with the other –
The sorcerer that Shakespeare deified,
The tempest that became the wreck of me...

My thoughts are in my arms and in my hands –
I conjure the fates – the destiny of love –
The power that can destroy and then create –
My daughter in the arms of Ferdinand...
And to this end – the mission's magic moves
To this beginning – the powers I reinstate.

Ariel-Prospero-Caliban, 2012 – 50" X 42"

LXXXV

ARIEL-PROSPERO-CALIBAN

The spirit of Sycorax hides behind
A fan of tortoiseshell – behind a fan
Issued from a hand that has no arm...
Where Ariel is trapped – inside his mind –
That lies exhausted on his other hand –
Imprisoned by the cruelty of her Charm...

Prospero – exiled from the world as is –
Frees his spirit – tangled in the limbs –
But still enslaves, and bends him to his will...
The ectoplasmic sphere he balances
Is subject to the antics of his whims –
The curious powers – ultra-magical...

Blake can play the role of Caliban –
Adept as he is at being no one's slave...
Prospero does not require his power –
Knows the rebellious knave is only human –
Someone to conjure, someone to deprave,
Someone to taste his rapturous elixir...

On The Isle of Prospero, 2012 – 38"X36"

LXXXVI

ON THE ISLE OF PROSPERO

Ensilvered in my eyes, the globe is blue –
The sun is in the night – the moon in day...
And as we ride astride the quiet goat,
The three of me beside the three of you –
Tranquil in the waters of the bay –
We sense the tide and feel its rhythms float

Into the sky, whose deep black shapes the blue –
Our feet upon the shell-less silken sands –
The waves of light, the planets that we touch –
While ocean swells emote this subtle hue,
The magic spells the matter in our hands –
The tidal light – the planets move so much...

Prospero is the sandman of the stars...
The diamond seeds he sprinkles in the air
Illumine in the water's blue translucence –
The fluid light – the potion in the spheres...
And as I ride with you – you're everywhere...
I kiss your beauty – deep in all of this ....

Titania Awakens To Bottom, 2012 – 50"X 42"

LXXXVII

TITANIA AWAKENS TO BOTTOM... MIDSUMMER NIGHT'S DREAM

Bottom has been changed into an Ass –
Asleep beside the memories of dreams –
Hopes that float away without a thought...
So why should he awaken beside a goddess,
If what it is is not quite what it seems,
If love can never be what it is not?

Titania fell into a potion's spell...
When she awoke the first she saw she loved –
Even this mortal ass – by happenstance...
The sense it makes is pure nonsensical...
Cheek to cheek, the better half is halved...
Love is a dream that's better left to chance...

Even if for a day or for an hour –
If for a time that does not end in time –
If for a mortal minute or if for never –
If out of weakness or if out of power...
They can not know that love is just a dream –
But when they wake they'll know it for forever...

Hamlet's Father's Ghost, 2012 – 50" X 42"

LXXXVIII

HAMLET'S FATHER'S GHOST

There is a mold in heaven here tonight –
That seeps through the aether – dampening my bones –
Chilling the castle walls – the bells bells bells –
That clamor whistles through the tower of night,
Knelling the death of fathers through the stones,
Listening as he reveals to me his hells...

The treachery of the Queen – his concubine –
Who poisoned his ear – complicit in the murder –
And father – just a whoremonger – in the end...
Unspeakable death – the horror of the crime –
As there will never be another father –
And madness rounds the corners of my mind...

So I, the whoreson, hear his howlings rage...
The death of him is like the death of me...
His ghost portends the dire ephiphany –
That I am the Death and Life of every stage...
That I am the act, the actor – to set free
These spectral chains – while dying endlessly...

The Madness Of Ophelia, 2012 – 50"X42"

LXXXIX

THE MADNESS OF OPHELIA

You will not live to see me kill the king...
My Claudius is your Polonius...
The fool who hid himself behind the curtain
Was not the one that I intended killing –
The death of fathers is the death of us.
Your love is madness, certain and uncertain –

And as I pierced the curtain – it's a shroud –
No life will come of us – my virgin princess –
Only the death of kings and sorry princes...
This globe is a theater of a deadly crowd...
So fly away – I'll leave you to your madness –
The ramblings of your incoherent voices...

The sadness of the willow breaks the bough,
And drops you in a brook of drunken water
That cools the heat – bipolar – in your head.
O why would you live if you do not know how?
And I am now the husband of disaster –
And all is death until all death is dead.

King Lear With Edgar And Tom The Fool, 2012 – 50" X 42"

LXXXX

KING LEAR WITH EDGAR AND FOOL

Upon the fiery heath with wind and rain
And bloodied eyes blinded by hearts of ice –
Roars the tempest – a lion in the clouds...
Vision bleeds through portals of the brain
The sanguine sense of nonsense – more or less –
And beggars' tatters clothe a funeral shroud –

As Bedlam rules the trials of sanity,
The coxcombed fool is bathed in disbelief...
The once great King can not see the seer –
His madness makes the truth his enemy –
The tragic muse weeps histories of grief,
And utter blindness makes his vision clear...

His kingdom has come of ruin and of rain –
As blind hallucinations sear his sight,
His trembling fingers reach for Edgar's skin –
Whose kindness entertains the mad king's pain...
So soon will come the calling of the night –
The voices in the tempest hear his vision.

King Lear And Fool, 2011 – 50"X 42"

LXXXXI

KING LEAR AND FOOL

Good father, I am furthered by your humour –
That is – the way you are before you were –
And both of us-together – passed the stages...
This madness has no syntax – just a fervor –
We know that we'd incur what would occur –
The dog days – the inventions of Hell's mages...

This heath is just a subterranean shelf
That's perched before the chasm of the sea,
From which we can be true to one another –
The white cliffs where we launch the ships of self
Into the voids of blind vacuity –
Even if what we see is just each other...

Rage against the wind, the rain, the fire,
And all the madness seeping saturates –
The thickness that emits from eyes and throat,
And leap from a ledge onto a funeral pyre,
That stirs the sky with tempests of the spirits
That otherwise our underworlds emote.

In The Home Of The Magician, 1986 – 48" X 32"

LXXXXII

IN THE HOME OF THE MAGICIAN

A decadent transformed into a pope,
And from his papal chair a tri-part flame
That lights the underskin that she exposed
Where she floats; the disparate eyes of hope,
The magic of the Mage who has no name,
Whose face is never seen – but just supposed –

Are fixed upon the focus of those gathered
To witness the levitation of the flesh,
The seance of the Mystics of Desire...
A flare excites the light of antimatter,
The particles of light the eyes enmesh,
And sew into the air the breath of fire...

The lovers assume the spirits and resume
The cyclic gravitation – pleasure's pose...
The curtain is drawn, the serpent moves away...
The magic stirs the phosphors in the room
That mesmerize the moments that he froze
With brush and light – the unseen face of day...

A Misplaced Tenor With A Displaced Soprano And Ectoplasm, 2016 – 42"X 40"

LXXXXIII

MISPLACED TENOR, DISPLACED SOPRANO AND ECTOPLASMIC MUSE IN ORANGE PANELED SPACE

There were two panels made of orange fire
That forged the clouds aglow behind the three,
Who sang an aria – sacrosanct and bright –
And whosoever listened to this choir
Heard whatever made their symphony –
A music formed from notes of orange light...

An ectoplasmic veil of flesh and dream
Converged behind a ball of crystal rose –
A platinum penance offered to the sun –
So gold and silver both began to stream
Into the notes the inspirations chose
Before the spirits sang the light to vision...

See the she-birds sing the songs of light –
The tenor of the notes resounds majestic,
The tortoise-shells fan the embers amorous,
As orange and silver redefine the night,
And displaced voices mesmerize the music
That issues from them – even as from us.

Ectoplasmic Flora, 2009 – 30" X 25"

LXXXXIV

ECTOPLASMIC FLORA

Flora holds the ectoplasmic sphere:
A bulb that glows translucent in the day,
Bringing the saffrons, indigoes to light –
Entwined in the garlands – spirits of the ear –
Music that color makes from yesterday –
Tomorrow just a passage through tonight...

Sweet alyssum – woven with golden currant –
The million bells – beside the trumpet vine –
The poplars in the heavens of the leaves –
The showers of light upon the clapboards vibrant –
The fragrant steps now sweet with columbine –
The confluence of colors – nature's weaves...

If flesh and light could ever prove a spirit
Is easy as a negligee to see –
And if the flowers startle it all alive –
Then the spirit veil she openly emits
Is solid as this light – this clarity
And as its spring, her flowers will survive.

Summoning Madame Blavatsky, 2009 – 30"X 42"

LXXXXV

SUMMONING MADAME BLAVATSKY

Were I to call the spirit of the spirits
Somewhere in the journey of the sky,
Elizabeth as Flora would be present,
Perhaps because as one they're closer to it
Than anything that saturates my eye...
Nature is a force that's evanescent,

And as this world is just antinomies:
Man as woman – woman as man – and God
Near the edge of space and its diffractions
Into the vested hope of inquiries
That I can only see as blue and red,
The spirit at the moment of sensation,

When synthesis from formless to a form
Is present in the beautiful sublime,
And hope a vector made of flowers and hands...
Into the light the child of hope is born –
Reasonless explanations without rhyme –
Only the beauty beauty understands.

The Metaphysician and Monsignor, 2010 – 50"X 42"

LXXXXVI

THE METAPHYSICIAN AND MONSIGNOR

The Metaphysician heard the word of God –
Juggled the clear-blue spheres upon his hands,
Open to the hand that cast the spirit
Into the ectosphere the Muse had heard,
As fine soft veils that rustled in the wind
That blew – before the Monsignor could hear it –

From the song that came from outer reaches
Into the voice that only she could sing...
Melody and music are the height of Art –
The hand of God unveiled the word he preaches,
Only so he invokes what she is singing
Which was the question answered at the start –

That light was made at first to fit a sound
That came from the nether-void at once to be
A message and a messenger – a choice –
That from no higher octave could be found –
The prayers that cycle this pure energy
In revelations – voice to voice to voice.

Artist And Ectoplasmic Ingres, 2010 – 50"X 36"

LXXXXVII

ARTIST AND ECTOPLASMIC INGRES

for Stephen Curtis

There never was a master, just a student –
So why should I betray myself with thought –
There is no one divine who still is living –
(Nothing that is not now is not evident) –
Life has been the master that has taught
That love, respect, exist in not one being,

Yet – everything around me is divine –
Whatever it is that would malign, corrupt,
Destroy the beauty and truth that is of me,
Perhaps in a poisoned cup of bloody wine,
That as it's tasted tries to interrupt
My mediations of joy and ecstasy –

Yet – Ingres is my model and my heart,
And in his spirit I can turn away
From things that terrify my sense of love,
And make idyllic only the truth of art,
'The utmost for the highest', nor betray
What those around me cannot know to give.

Poet And Ectoplasm, 2010 – 50"X 42"

LXXXXVIII

POET AND ECTOPLASM

for Antonio Alfredo Giarraputo

He sat beside the specters and the spheres,
With orbs of crystal glowing in the air,
As its reflections hovered, rose, descended,
And made a dance of light of atmosphere –
A subtle stream that laid his shadow bare –
Young blind Homer held him – hand in hand...

The Pipes of Pan were silent in his ear,
But still the notes became a panegyric,
Lauding the spirit that heard the spirits sing
Compassionate verses – Aristotle-clear –
Heart and mind combined in matters epic –
He knew, in depth, the soul of everything...

From the ectoplasmic realm he summoned
The warmth and touch of all that he divined,
As if a mystic sphere endowed his knowledge
With all the sustenance he had consumed,
And shared as a light of universal mind –
A hope – a guide – a friend – a privilege.

Marcel Duvinci, 2010 – 50"X 42"

LXXXXIX

MARCEL DUVINCI

The cubes that I created were a chapel
Into which tiny spheres of thought devolved
Into historical means of de-perspective,
So I could please the spatial citadel
From which the eye of overview evolved,
Or bring new life to things that do not live...

Whoever has opinions has whatever
Is needed to make the necessary gauche,
So from the mental drain my spirit ran
Into the clear pure ectoplasmic river
Hanging from God's right hand – the rivers rush –
And Leonardo his ectoplasmic man...

Why not carve up bodies to see the veins –
Or make myself the mother that once I was –
Or drape myself in machinations of time?
I changed the age of art and so its brains –
And made the trends that idiots call laws –
While spirits in the temple strike the chimes.

The Displaced Soprano Sings Into The Light, 2016 – 42"X 40"

EPILOGUE

SINGING INTO THE LIGHT

First and last, let's pause to praise the singers, who stayed forever just to hear one song, and one that ran through images of mages, saints and demons, Pan-esque poses deep in faun-filled forests, effusive streams of ectoplasmic blues, lovebirds who appeared again, again, again, and then again, poets intercepting muse-made missives, Shakespeare and his madness and despair, and all the while the mischief of the maker, Donald Langosy, who puzzled with his queries and connections, and moved us where magic delved, where saintly fortune tellers, removed from Dante's pains, were given credence and complete forgiveness. Yes – let's start where we end, before the place where there is no beginning, where only the quiet light can resonate our raptures and make our words like brush strokes in the night – tiny stars that rivet ears and eyes, that move outward – ever outward – as sunlight will not end once past the earth and singing will not stop to see the sun!

— ERIC SIGLER

AN AFTERWORD FROM TODD SWIFT

I should start by making a claim so outlandish it is a pleasure. That is that this book is either a work of genius, or hogwash. If it is hogwash, then there are at least two culprits to blame for the hoax – Langosy and Sigler – and it seems unlikely to me that two sensitive, intelligent, creative people could ally themselves with Eyewear to astonish the reading public with rubbish.

So that leaves us with the bizarre spectacle of these extraordinary paintings – ghoulish, post-modern, classical, romantic – at once hilarious, erotic, zany, deeply learned, crazed, and terrifying – that seem to present a fusion of all the plastic art of the past two thousand years – while also simultaneously offering a very original and peculiar personal take on this broad swathe of human creative history. The book is not just a gallery or a gathering, it is a museum – of sacrilegious, pious, pagan and profane characters, from all walks of life, and all shelves of the library. Not even Yeats was this allusive, let alone Auden.

And this is before Sigler repeats the impossible. For I have come to consider these 100 or so paintings as impossibly bizarre and brilliant. Their passion, insight, and wit is remarkable – yet they admit of being in no school or style that has ever been fashionable these past 50 years or more. But nor is this pastiche, or knock-off. If it is simply droll, then so was Welles. No, the art is deeply informed serious play – a cry of purposeful revaluation of beauty and its bumpkins.

Then comes Sigler. No poet has ever quite done what he has done here. These are not merely ekphrastic works. These are stylistically mature, very intelligent, poems, in a long series, directly deepening the response to each of the paintings, interpreting them, responding to them, but never piggy-backing on them. Both artists do the heavy lifting here, all the time. What we get is the double whammy of a painting, then a poem, that bear seriously one upon the other, regardless of which was temporally prior in the causal sequence.

In other words, if Sigler's is the supposedly critical intelligence here, reviewing the paintings and offering a riposte, his is also a supremely imaginative and creative response.

What a picaresque tale these poems tell. It feels as if (indeed it is) all the greatest characters or figures from mythology, Shakespeare, fairy tales, and European writing, appear in these poems, sometimes terrifyingly reincarnated as The Roosterman or The Prom Queen. America and Grimm combine in a way that might make Lynch flinch in awe or fear.

What of the poetry, as poetry?

Well, it is impressive. The poetry, as you will see pretty quickly, uses a lot of metre and rhyme. The form is regular. In that way, it is traditional. But the poems are not conservative – they are anarchic, romantic, Blakean.

The diction and style of the poems, at first, seems elegant, polished, stiff... But as one gets into the play between the eccentric worlds of the images, and the texts, one discovers an eruption of permissive, daemonic energy, that recalls, more than Poe and his artifice, the imaginative gift-giving of a Whitman.

This is a new classic of creative American expression – homely at times, self-taught, and ruggedly idiosyncratic, even as it is cooperative. In teamwork, these two creators have established a new benchmark, it seems to me, for out-sized vision and effort in the field of poetic testimony – even testament.

Lay this book beside The Classics, Dante, Shakespeare, the King James Bible, *Moby Dick*... it has the gloomy, wild, and oceanic heft of such works. It makes vast claims about art, love, life, desire, death, comedy, pathos, and creation itself. This book does what no one asked for – it has belatedly introduced major new voices into a canon, shifting each other's work around it in the process, as large as America and all literature, as brazen as love or friendship. I hail and welcome this beautiful, strange book, even as I recoil from its claims on me.

It says nothing new, perhaps, and it says what it says often in archaic, weird, uncanny ways... But then, I glance again, and it says this as never before, and so well.

Dr Todd Swift
Writer-in-residence Pembroke College, Cambridge University
England, 2017